LITERATURE IN THE THEATRE

LITERATURE IN THE THEATRE

AND OTHER ESSAYS

BY

W. A. DARLINGTON

Essay Index Reprint Series

BOOKS FOR LIBRARIES PRESS, INC.
FREEPORT, NEW YORK

First Published 1925
Reprinted 1968

LIBRARY OF CONGRESS CATALOG NUMBER:
68-16924

PRINTED IN THE UNITED STATES OF AMERICA

To

MY MOTHER

AUTHOR'S NOTE

All but one of the essays which make up this book appeared in their original form either in the *Fortnightly Review* or in the *Daily Telegraph*. For purposes of publication in the present volume they have been freely altered, rearranged, and in many cases re-written.

CONTENTS

PLAYS AND BOOKS (*Continued*)

STAGE AND STUDY

LITERATURE IN THE THEATRE

I HAVE headed this essay "Literature in the Theatre" rather than "Literature in Drama" because I want to make it quite clear from the outset that I am writing as a playgoer. In my opinion plays cannot be judged, at all events with any approach to finality, except in their relation to the playhouse; and no dramatic composition which loses effect by being staged, however fine a piece of writing it may be, has any real right to rank as a good play. And so, since "Drama" is a wide term which may be held to describe any and every composition which is cast in the form of dialogue and divided into acts and scenes (such as Mr. Hardy's *The Dynasts*, which was never intended for stage production at all), I have sought to define the issue by choosing a less general term for my title. In the theatre, at any rate, plays are plays first and "literary" compositions (that is, reading matter) afterwards. The theatre is like a sieve, through which only those plays may pass which conform to the theatre's requirements; and you find a heterogeneous collection indeed slipping safely through the meshes—*Hamlet* and *Charley's Aunt, The Cherry Orchard* and *Chu Chin Chow, The Doll's House* and *East Lynne, Peter Pan* and *Sweet Lavender* and *The Cabaret Girl*. And in the heap that the sieve has rejected you will find much drama of great literary worth—Mr. Gordon Bottomley's *Britain's Daughter*, for instance, and Miss Dane's *Will Shakespeare*, and many another. With these I am not here concerned.

If "Drama" is a wide term, "Literature" is a wider. I suppose that you and I and all the rest have, each of us, some hazy idea what we mean when we use the word; but few of us mean quite the same thing, and still fewer mean anything exact at all. Therefore, if a discussion of the place of literature in the theatre is to have any value, we must first have before us some definition, as broad as possible, of what we are to understand the word to mean. Choosing such a definition is rather a delicate business, but I suggest the following to be going on with: "Literature is the name we give to any writing which attains to a high artistic standard." It may be possible—or, indeed, necessary—to narrow this down later on; but meanwhile I do not believe that anybody will dissent from it except those benighted people (political agents and propagandists in particular) to whom "literature" signifies "any form of printed matter."

There is a strong and influential body of opinion which holds that literature has no prescriptive right in the theatre at all. Those who maintain this view are enthusiasts of the playhouse—or, to use their own honourable term, "men of the theatre." They consider that while a fine play may very easily *contain* literature, it cannot in its nature *be* literature; that its literary qualities are secondary and incidental.

The first argument they are accustomed to bring forward is, put briefly, that plays are written entirely in dialogue; that is, in the language of ordinary speech. Therefore, since people while using ordinary speech do not talk in a literary way, a bald record of their speech cannot be literature. Conversely, the instant your characters begin to "talk literary" they cease to use the language of ordinary life and become unconvincing and undramatic. This argument is not new, of course. More than ten years ago Mr. C. E. Montague made an exhaustive inquiry[1] into the matter. He quoted, to begin with, two statements which embodied the opposing views in their extreme form—this, from the pen of the late H. D. Traill: "Of every drama, as we moderns understand the term, it may, I hold, be affirmed that, though some of them may, and do, contain great literature, they are, to the extent to which they are literary, undramatic, and, to the extent to which they are dramatic, unliterary"[2]; and this, from a contemporary dramatist (not named): "To tell an interesting or amusing story through the medium of dialogues which appear to be the natural speech of human beings—that *is* literature."

From Mr Montague's investigation into this "tangle of cross-meanings" I shall have occasion to quote more than once. Indeed, I foresee that I shall have to fight hard against the temptation to quote from it far too freely; for Mr. Montague is a writer who imposes his particular way of saying things upon you so that you forget that there can be any other; and I must perforce go over much of the

[1] "The Literary Play" (English Association Essays, 1911).

[2] This sentence might do good service to a grammarian as an illustration of the use of the comma.

ground that his essay covered. Mr. Montague, then, takes the notion that dialogue "is a bald record of human speech," and, after a minute examination, decides that it will not do. The gist of his conclusions is contained in the following passage[1]:— "The 'real life' which a dramatist like Mr. Galsworthy is sometimes supposed merely to take as he finds it, and to give out as he takes it, does just about as much to help him as a piano manufacturer does for a composer. It gives him every note he wants; he has only, it may be said, to take the notes he sees and put them in an order. But it certainly does not need less craft cunning, or a less profoundly-felt emotion, to string together a few tags and ends of ready-made Cockney speech into the police court scene in *The Silver Box* than it takes to string a few ready-made notes into the tune of a fine song. Even to put it in that way is to make too great a concession, for I used the word 'ready-made,' and a dramatist does not find even small fragments of his work ready-made for him before he begins."

Considerations of space compel me to state as a conclusion what Mr. Montague establishes by reasoning and example; but I do so without misgiving owing to my own complete conviction on the point, that a play may be literature not only in its "literary" passages, but in its swiftest and most dramatic moments also. I therefore go on to the second argument which the "man of the theatre" commonly advances—that plays are intended, in the first instance, to be spoken, literature to be read; and that the two methods of composition are so fundamentally

[1] "The Literary Play," p. 83.

different as to be mutually exclusive. This particular point of view was forcibly expressed and illustrated in a letter which I once received from the famous American actor, Mr. James K. Hackett. I had published an article stating my conviction (already mentioned) that plays must be judged on the stage and not in the study; and Mr. Hackett felt impelled to write and tell me how strongly he agreed with the views I had expressed. But, as will appear, he went further in that direction than I could feel prepared to accompany him.

"Your view of the acted and unacted drama," wrote Mr. Hackett, "is absolutely sound, and it should not be questioned by any man of practical experience." He proceeded to cite in corroboration an incident in his own college life, when he competed for a much sought after oratory medal. "In the case of orations it was necessary to write them first and then submit them to the English department. . . . At the expiration of a few weeks I was summoned to the professor's *sanctum sanctorum*, and a conversation on these lines took place. He said: 'My dear Hackett, how a man of your intelligence can write such utter twaddle and rot as you have written in this so-called oration is beyond my comprehension. It is rot, plain, unadulterated rot, and if I am on the platform when you deliver it I shall mark you zero. There is not a literary line in it, nor a line that is fit to remember or re-read.' I said, 'My dear Professor, I have made no attempt to write a literary effusion. This is an *oration*. I wrote this to *deliver by word of mouth,* not to be read in the quiet of your study. . . . Have you not, sir, with your experience, realized that drama is not literature, nor literature drama? Neither is oratory literature. In one you must make your effects by momentary strokes, in the other you make them by the printed page, which can be studied and re-studied at length, if necessary.' The professor informed me that I was a very immature and iconoclastic young man, and he repeated that he would mark me zero if he were present when I delivered the oration." (As it fell out, the professor was ill on the momentous day, and the young iconoclast won the medal with a record mark.) "I personally think," says Mr. Hackett later in the same letter, "that one of the greatest faults that the dramatist falls into is to have his effusion printed and published and circulated as literature."

These extracts (which I print here with Mr. Hackett's very kind permission) seem to me to put the case for the man of the theatre as fully as it need be put. But I cannot agree with the conclusion. Mr. Hackett was undoubtedly right to compose his oration in a form different from that of the essay which his professor seems to have expected of him (incidentally, his realization of this fact at so early an age goes far to account for his success in his profession); what he does not appear to realize, or admit, is that the composition would have had an equal chance in either form of being literature. I may be forgiven, perhaps, for suggesting that the professor's estimate of Mr. Hackett's "effusion" may have been more just than the young iconoclast could perceive, and that the subsequent high marking by a tribunal of dons who had not read the oration was a tribute less to Mr. Hackett's powers as a writer of speeches than to the gifts as a speaker which have since brought him fame. Demosthenes, Cicero, and Burke all wrote their speeches with an eye to delivery, not publication; yet to none of the three is an important place in the hierarchy of literature denied on that account.

At all events, let us hear Mr. Montague on the same point[1]:—"There is another fairly obvious precaution that the writer of a play meant for acting should take. He has to do what is sometimes called in the trade, 'getting out of the way of the acting.' As a rule, when a scene acts well, it is not that the actors express over again in pantomime just what the author expresses in his words; that would give an effect of over-acting; but it is just as likely in such cases that the author has over-written as that the actors are over-acting. What the more skilful dramatist consciously does is to divide the opportunities for expressiveness between his actors and himself. Of all the things that he would set down on paper if he were writing a piece of dialogue simply to be read, as in a novel, he will leave a large proportion out in order that the actor may have these significances to convey in his own way. . . . When this mapping out of the relative shares in the final accomplishment of the acted play has been adroitly done, the mere text of a play will often look scrappy or disjointed to a reader who does not bring to it the special theatrical imagination.[2] When *Hedda*

[1] "The Literary Play," pp. 76-78.

[2] Compare with this a remark of Mr. Granville Barker's: "I have seen a performance of Tchekov's *Cherry Orchard* in Moscow and to read the play afterwards was like reading the libretto of

Gabler was first read and seen acted in England, a very capable literary critic candidly said that when he read it he could not make out what it all meant, but when he saw it on the stage it was as clear as crystal. One can hardly imagine a revolution of that completeness brought about in an educated person's mind by the first night of a play of Tennyson or Browning. What happens in this case is rather that what was fully expressed in the bare text seems to labour in its own clearness on the stage. . . . When a theatre manager reads a new play and finds in it this lack of provision for the actor's share in the joint work, he may naturally say to himself that here is some precious literary man trying to write plays without knowing the game, and he may briefly describe such plays as 'literary' plays. . . . The definition does not go very deep. It only means that some writer has not conformed to the conditions imposed by a particular kind of writing. That is to say, it means that some literary person has not been literary enough." And again : " In a shrewd man of the theatre like Ibsen, you find scenes of the most concentrated dialogue diluted with idle-looking little trivialities, perhaps about cigarettes or coffee, odds and ends that may look futile or superfluous when you read them in the text. And, on the other hand, when a too drastically compressed play like Mr. Stephen Phillips's *Paolo and Francesca* is acted . . . you have a sensation that passages of

an opera—missing the music. Great credit to the actors; no discredit to Tchekov. For—and this is what the *undramatic* writer so fails to understand—with the dramatist the words on paper are but the seeds of the play." The *Exemplary Theatre*, footnote to p. 229.

much beauty and importance are slipping past you before you can fairly grasp them. . . . Such a dramatist would not submit to the special conditions of the theatre and the platform, which force dramatists and orators to work their gold, like jewellers, with some alloy in it."

Poets and novelists often seem, when writing plays, purposely to neglect ordinary dramatic technique. The only reason I can suggest is that these men despise drama as a literary form because of its obvious limitations—as, in fact, Robert Louis Stevenson openly confessed that he did;[1] whereas they surely ought to embrace its limitations, as any poet does when he writes a sonnet. It is absurd to suppose that in any art you can have supreme expression without supreme mastery of your medium.

The conclusion towards which Mr. Montague's arguments all set, and, as I think, sweep the mind overwhelmingly away with them, is that only a general tendency to slovenly thinking on the meaning of the word "literature" could lead such a man as Traill to assert "that the right sort of handling for the study must of necessity be—cannot of its very nature help being—the wrong sort of handling for the stage." This is a statement so extreme that even the most unyielding opponent of literature on the stage might hesitate to subscribe to it; but Mr. Hackett's sweeping condemnation of the publication of plays is in much the same vein.

A third argument often used by the man of the theatre is that while you may often find passages in

[1] *Robert Louis Stevenson the Dramatist,* by Sir Arthur Pinero, p. 30.

plays of extreme literary beauty and worth, yet such passages will always turn out on close examination to have no dramatic value. The best, because at once the most strongly marked and the most widely known, evidence in support of this notion is produced from the works of the Elizabethan dramatists in general, and Shakespeare in particular. Passage after passage in Shakespeare's plays—including, perhaps, the majority of the most often quoted "bits"—can be, and are, dismissed by these critics as being mere undramatic chunks of superb poetry arbitrarily inserted into the text of the plays. They leave you to infer that if you were to weed out of the text of, say, *Hamlet* every line that does not directly help the dramatic action, you would have a play which, while certainly dramatic, would not be literary. I will return to this point later. For the moment my preoccupation is with the extracted "literary passages."

About these there is just one pregnant question to be asked—Do they, or do they not, serve any dramatic purpose? You may possibly decide this question in favour of one or two passages because they assist in the delineation of character; that is merely to beg the question, since in such case they ought never to have been extracted—but who is to judge with any finality on such a point? Take one such passage, Polonius' advice to Laertes. Mr. A. B. Walkley, in *Drama and Life,* treats this particular speech as pure literary digression on the part of the dramatist. "Shakespeare himself," he says, "had these characteristics, and sought expression for them on the stage without a perpetual solicitude for consistency or intelligibility in his mouthpiece. A father is addressing his son starting on a journey. Shakespeare sees the 'good things' appropriate to the situation in general, and at once puts them in the mouth of Polonius, though it suits him afterwards to make Polonius a 'tedious old fool.'" There you have one man's view of the speech; and another man—Professor Gilbert Norwood—disagrees with it so violently that he quotes the above sentences from Mr. Walkley's book and remarks, "In a passage like this we may watch the art of dramatic criticism committing suicide."[1] I propose to leave any disputed passages on one side, then, and to consider only extracts such as Professor Norwood himself admits do not assist either dramatic action or character-building; for example, the "Queen Mab" speech of Mercutio, or the "equally exquisite description of the bees' commonwealth in *Henry the Fifth*."[2]

Professor Norwood explains such passages as being signs of a transition from lyric into drama. This is an ingenious explanation, but not, I think, the right one. "No one doubts," he says, "that such disquisitions are brought in only to gratify the sense of literary beauty, and with no thought of the plot." Here I agree, except with the word "only." Perhaps there was no thought of the *plot* in Shakespeare's mind when he wrote these passages; indeed, there hardly can have been any. But that is surely not the point—which is, whether he wrote them "*only* to gratify the sense of literary beauty,"

[1] *Euripides and Shaw*, pp. 143-44.
[2] *Ibid.*, pp. 156-57. *Henry V*, I, 2.

or had besides that some thought of the *play*. To that question I answer unhesitatingly that these passages certainly do serve a very definite dramatic purpose. They did for the Elizabethan audience exactly what the work of the scenic artist does for the audience of to-day—they supplied decoration. Every man of the theatre admits—rather, trumpets abroad—the great and increasing importance of decoration in play production. And yet settings and lights and colours and clothes have nothing to do with the plot of the play they adorn. They are partly the means by which we satisfy the human being's perpetual hunger for beauty, and partly the means by which we produce "atmosphere." For humanity, to the perpetual despair of its handful of idealists, cannot assimilate its drama neat. This is true of everybody, from that complacent target of scorn the Tired Business Man (whose deplorable taste calls for one halfpennyworth of drama to an intolerable deal of crude beauty, as supplied by musical comedy) up through the animal kingdom to the high-browed idealist himself, who is only able to endure stark drama because he has taught his senses to perceive and appreciate beauties of wisdom and observation, form and workmanship, which may lurk beneath deliberate ugliness of subject and character.

The effects which our modern producers obtain through the eyes of the spectators, Shakespeare and his contemporaries had to get by appealing through the ears of their audiences to the sense of literary beauty of which Professor Norwood speaks. How they succeeded, much magnificent poetry still lives to bear witness. In fact, the scope thus offered to purely poetical genius attracted to the Elizabethan stage men little suited to dramatic writing; men like Marlowe, of whom even so great an admirer as Professor Saintsbury says, "It is impossible to call Marlowe a great dramatist. . . . Marlowe was one of the great poets of the world whose work was cast by accident and caprice into an imperfect mould of drama."[1] But if his drama was imperfect, the splendour of its decoration has not been surpassed. This decorative stuff is everywhere in Shakespeare, too; you can hardly open him at random without your eye being caught by some rich jewel of poetry which, from the strictly dramatic point of view, need not be there. In many cases, of course, the poetry actually takes the place of scenery by deliberate word-painting. Such is the wonderful description of the still starlit night in Portia's garden,[2] and such are the seeming casual touches which pervade *The Tempest,* so that the mind is led to conceive for itself an island whose enchantment is far more potent than any that the art of the scene-painter can suggest. For example:

> "Be not afear'd; the isle is full of noises,
> Sounds and sweet airs, that give delight and hurt not.
> Sometimes a thousand twangling instruments
> Will hum about mine ears, and sometimes voices
> That, if I then had waked after long sleep
> Will make me sleep again . . ."[3]

It would take a bold man to set out to match that with a pot of paint and a strip of canvas.

This—if I may here be allowed to digress for a

[1] *Elizabethan Literature,* by Professor Saintsbury, pp. 78-79.
[2] *Merchant of Venice,* V, i.
[3] *The Tempest,* III, ii.

moment—is the strongest argument I know of against elaborate, or at any rate realistic, production of Shakespeare.[1] Take the scene in Portia's garden. If Lorenzo, speaking against a black curtain or a conventional background, says—

"How sweet the moonlight sleeps upon this bank"

the imagination of every spectator who has ever seen moonlight is set free to reproduce for itself its own conception of the scene. If he says it on a dim stage, where the bank and the moonlight are suggested and no more, the imagination is neither impeded nor (unless it is sluggish) very materially helped. But if he sits on a conscientious, practicable canvas bank and rhapsodizes about the moonlight pouring down upon him from the electrician's perch, imagination departs altogether; all we feel is that Lorenzo is a thundering liar. And so Shakespeare in realistic settings has too often the effect which Mr. Montague speaks of in Browning and Tennyson—of elaborating his own clearness. The last West End revival of *The Tempest*—Miss Tree's at the Aldwych in February, 1921—illustrated this point rather aptly, because it was decorated in two quite different styles. Most of

[1] Oscar Wilde, expressing approval of the elaborate settings of Irving's *Much Ado* and Wilson Barrett's *Hamlet* in the *Dramatic Review* forty years ago, indulged in speculation as to what Shakespeare's own attitude in the matter would have been. He decided that Shakespeare would have preferred to have had scenery; that he felt cramped without it, and resented having to achieve his effects by means of poetical description. This is probable enough, but it is beside the mark; because, as a matter of hard fact, Shakespeare *did* get his effects by means of description, and the producer who makes his scenery serve the same purpose renders the descriptions tautologous, and ought logically to omit them.

the island scenes, painted in a frankly non-realistic style by Mr. Hugo Rumbold, rather helped than hindered the descriptive passages of the poetry in their function of creating atmosphere. Then came a sea-shore scene painted by a clever and efficient practitioner of the realistic school. He had evidently set out to paint a pretty picture, taking for his inspiration " Come unto these yellow sands." They *were* yellow! They reminded me of those jolly posters which explain that Skegness (or somewhere) is So Bracing. The whole setting only needed a pier and a band to be perfect; but exactly what Prospero and Ariel were doing in such a milieu did not seem too easy to understand.

So much for the " extraneous " literature in plays —the passages with which Traill admitted you might " butter " a drama and so give it an illusory appearance of being itself literature. With the rise of the decorative side of the art of the theatre such " buttering " has dropped more and more out of fashion. Next comes the problem, how far a play in which the author attends strictly and strongly to his first purpose—of making a vehicle for acting—can be literature. Before going on to examine this point more closely, let me return for one moment, as I said I should, to *Hamlet* and ask one question. Supposing you were to take *Hamlet* and denude it of every scrap of extraneous poetry—of every line, that is, which does not either assist the action of the play or your necessary understanding of the characters; could you possibly say of the great acting play thus obtained that it was not still great poetry? If you could, then so far as you are concerned my argument fails, and any argument I am likely to adduce will fail. But if you agree that *Hamlet* is as certainly great poetry in its dramatic passages as in its merely poetic passages (whichever they may be), then it is clear that if Shakespeare could achieve literature with a good acting play, then any other writer of a good acting play may, if his writing reaches the necessary artistic level, have achieved literature likewise. At this point, I think, we begin to feel an imperative need for some closer investigation into what "literature" really is, to replace the very broad definition which I adopted at the beginning of this essay. I took it, you remember, because I did not want to start off upon a note of controversy; and now it will not carry us any further. Up to this point we have regarded "literature" merely as signifying writing of a high order. All literature is fine writing, sure enough; but there is much fine writing which fails to be literature. Fine writing is only literature when it is the verbal expression of fine thinking; whenever, and in proportion as, it expresses fine thought, writing becomes literature. The users of the word "literature" often do not take this into consideration. We use the phrase "literary critic" to denote a man who criticizes books, and to distinguish him from a "dramatic critic," who deals with plays. But this is only a superficial use of the word, having reference to technique rather than art, expression of an idea rather than the idea itself, style rather than matter; and technique, expression, style in literature is nothing more than an indispensable adjunct, inseparable from matter because dependent upon it both for its existence and its form. "Style," wrote

Coleridge,[1] "is, of course, nothing else but the art of conveying the meaning appropriately and with perspicuity, whatever that meaning may be, and one criterion of style is that it shall not be translatable without injury to the meaning." A century later Mr. Arnold Bennett firmly elaborated the same idea.[2] "Style," he says, "cannot be distinguished from matter. When a writer conceives an idea he conceives it in a form of words. That form of words constitutes his style, and it is absolutely governed by the idea. The idea can only exist in words, and it can only exist in one form of words. You cannot say exactly the same thing in two different ways. Slightly alter the expression, and you slightly alter the idea. . . . A writer, having conceived and expressed an idea, may, and probably will, 'polish it up.' But what does he polish up? To say that he polishes up his style is merely to say that he is polishing up his idea, that he has discovered faults or imperfections in his idea and is perfecting it. An idea exists in proportion as it is expressed; it exists when it is expressed, and not before." From this it follows that when your fine idea achieves complete expression in words it is literature. It is equally literature in whichever of the different forms of expression it may be cast—that of a book, a poem, a speech, a play. But it is also obvious that your idea must suit the particular form in which it is to be expressed, and suit it exactly; otherwise, in the process of expression it becomes mangled into another idea, something like your original idea, but less fine,

[1] *Essays*, Everyman Edition, p. 325.
[2] *Literary Taste*, p. 44.

and therefore not literature. An idea which achieves perfect expression as a sonnet, for instance, would probably make a very imperfect four-act play. An idea which is literature as a novel may be maimed out of all semblance to itself when adapted for the stage.[1]

Supposing, then, we ask ourselves if there is any one class of ideas which is specially well fitted to expression in dramatic form; we can, I think, find an entirely satisfactory and definite answer. Let us apply the highest—the only final—test by which we can assess artistic values; the test of immortality. Books which attain to such a standard of achievement that they are constantly being rediscovered, and their rediscovery celebrated by what Mr. Arnold Bennett calls "The Passionate Few";[2] drama

[1] We have had a striking example of this quite recently in Joseph Conrad's play, *The Secret Agent.* The complete failure of this stage version when it was produced at the Ambassadors made a great many earnest people very angry. That a play by so great a writer as Conrad should receive only ten days' hearing was, we were told, one more dark blot on the already maculate scutcheon of the London stage. Some blamed the producer, some the actors, some the critics. But when you come down to plain facts, what was wrong was that Conrad had joined Tennyson, Browning and Stephen Phillips in Mr. Montague's category of writers who have not conformed to the traditions imposed by a particular kind of writing. His play retained too much of the form of his novel, because he was a great artist in the novel-form, and lacked enough experience of the stage to show him how different in form a play must be from a book. Sir James Barrie, with experience of both forms, makes no such mistake when he adapts from one to the other. The form of his play, *The Little Minister,* owes nothing to that of the book; nor does *Peter and Wendy* smack at all of the stage. This is because in both cases Barrie has taken his original erection entirely to pieces before beginning to build again on the old foundation. Conrad did not do this. And so, once more, "a literary person has not been literary enough."

[2] *Literary Taste,* pp. 19 *et seq.*

which the passionate few constantly insist on putting before the play-going public from generation to generation—such are the very aristocracy of the study and the stage. If we examine the dramatic masterpieces of past ages which have stood this test and are alive for the stage to-day, we find in them one common factor. No play that has lived has lacked this one essential quality—supreme delineation of human character. The primary reason for which a play is written is to provide a vehicle for acting; and acting expresses itself in terms of human nature, because the actor's medium is himself. Taste in ideas and in language are as subject to changes of fashion as taste in clothes or houses. Human nature, although it reacts differently to different environments and systems of education, remains the same in fundamentals. *Naturam expellas furca, tamen usque recurret.* The great playwright is he who, while making a true picture of a phase of the changeful surface of life, yet conveys a sense of his comprehension of changeless depths below. The cherished conventions of one generation are often the laughing-stock of the next; and no play whose author takes his stand upon merely conventional morality can possibly be literature, or can conceivably have more than a transitory life.

Look at the *Medea*. It is a great play, and great literature. It is alive for the stage to-day because Euripides was more interested in Medea herself and the secret places of her heart than he was in the conventions of his time. A smaller man would have believed in those conventions, according to which Jason was entirely within his rights to terminate his illegal union with a foreign woman[1] when the chance of marriage with a Greek princess presented itself. A smaller Euripides might well have upheld Jason instead of despising him. In that case his play might quite possibly have taken a first instead of a third prize at the time, and it would now have been dead, except to scholars, for over two thousand years. Consider a modern play, first-rate in technique but based largely on conventional morality —*The Second Mrs. Tanqueray*. If it were not that the drawing of Paula Tanqueray's character shows flashes of real insight and understanding, this play could never have had its recent very successful revival. Already the behaviour of everybody concerned, in the scenes where young Ardale's previous relations with Paula are discovered and discussed, rings utterly false. First Paula and Ardale, and then Tanqueray, assume as a fundamental fact of human nature that this discovery makes a marriage between Ardale and Ellean impossible; and Ellean, when she finds out the nature of the obstacle, meekly acquiesces. By allowing this complete unanimity among his characters the author makes it appear that in his view no other behaviour is humanly possible; to him it is inevitable that the lovers must part. To the present generation, however, this solution is far from inevitable; it is not even convincing. Conventions have changed. A modern Ellean would probably say that it was entirely for her to decide whether she would forgive

[1] Compare the attitude on the same point of Simo, who may be taken to represent the average sound Athenian citizen, in the *Andria* of Terence—a translation from Menander.

Ardale or forget him; her choice would depend, not on her father's idea of what was fitting, but on her own. She knew that Ardale had lived "a man's life"; the fact that her stepmother had been his companion need not of necessity make any difference to her feelings on the matter. It is quite possible that this play will die owing to the inability of future generations to understand what all the fuss was about, whereas if Sir Arthur Pinero had been able to discover how much of his theme depended on conventional and how much on essential morality—as Euripides did, and Ibsen and Mr. Shaw[1] have done—he too might have made a play which would have been not merely an effective piece of stage architecture, but literature of a high order as well.

Here, then, is my conclusion—that an acting play can certainly be great literature, but only when a great playwright has seen clear down into the depths of human nature, and has expressed simply and truthfully what he has seen. Marlowe may stand as a cautionary example. His plays lose caste as literature because[2] their characters are for the most part warped, exaggerated, inhuman. The poetry (by which I mean not only such admired passages as the apostrophe to Helen in *Doctor Faustus*, but the whole body of Marlowe's verse) lives and glows still. But this is not enough. Marlowe's compositions are like garments made out of lovely, shimmering stuff

[1] Mr. Shaw has occasionally been so busy getting outside the conventions of his time that he has forgotten to take human nature with him.

[2] At a recent production *The Jew of Malta* proved merely a beautiful curiosity, whose extraordinary bombast most of the actors were unable to handle except by burlesquing it.

which yet fail to fit their wearers for lack of skill in the cutting out. Euripides and Shakespeare—no greater poets, possibly, than Marlowe—stand far above him as literary artists for this one reason, that when they set out to write drama they understood the word to mean not poetry in dramatic form, but plays for the theatre.

PLAYS FROM NOVELS

It is a true saying, and worthy to be believed, that plays which are based upon or adapted from novels are seldom good plays. Any regular playgoer in London during the last few years has had many chances of testing the truth of the statement, for there has been a steady stream of stage versions of stories which first saw the light in novel form; and in all the number there have been only a few passable plays and hardly any good ones. Now, the turning of novels into plays is not going to stop. In the present condition of our theatre I do not see how it can possibly stop. The theatre to-day is very largely in the hands of men who, while possessing some of the qualities of the ideal impresario, lack the first and most essential of all—the courage of their convictions. Thanks to the high rents of playhouses and the increased cost of play-producing, they have lost their nerve, or at any rate their enterprise. Rather than face the risks which the exploitation of unknown talent necessarily involves and always has involved, they try to ensure success by importing quantities of plays which have already been tried out upon, and found popular with, the American or the French public. This is a miserable, pusillanimous policy; but it exists, and seems only too likely to endure—until, at least, time works some happy miracle to make the public tire obviously of imported food, or to lower costs, or to bring to the few courageous managements fortunes large enough to excite their merely commercial rivals to envy and imitation.

For the present, the policy has the inevitable result of drying up the supply of new plays. If an unknown man has a good story to tell, his chance of getting it published as a novel is immeasurably greater than his chance of getting it produced as a play; so he writes it as a novel, hoping that when he has made a name for himself in that sphere he will have a better chance in the theatre. Often enough, therefore, your young novelist is really a playwright who has been forced to approach his true calling by a roundabout route owing to the plain necessity of earning a living while he is trying to learn stage technique and to find a manager willing to risk capital on his work. There is little enough money in novel-writing, save for the fortunate few; but in play-writing there is none at all, save for the handful that are luckier still. If a man whose chief ambition is to write plays happens to be independent of what he earns in the theatre, he can afford to peg away at his play-writing, treating it as a hobby till success comes his way; but if he needs the money that his pen may bring in, play-writing is a luxury that he cannot afford. He must stick to novels, to short stories, to journalism until he has won his independence. Then he may turn to his true line; and his most obvious and easy way of doing so is to begin by dramatizing any of his own novels that may seem to be suitable for stage adaptation. Indeed, if he should chance to have written a novel of real popularity, he has the cheering knowledge that there is a public already made to give a stage version of his book a favourable hearing. This latter reflection does not appeal only to the novelist who *can* write plays; it also makes playwrights out of many popular novelists who have no special call whatever to write for the stage—except the knowledge that if a reasonably acceptable stage version can be manufactured out of (say) *The Way of an Eagle* or *Paddy the Next Best Thing,* the box-office receipts may bring in riches beyond the dreams even of popular novelists. No—the turning of novels into plays is certainly not going to stop; and therefore I am making this attempt to state the reasons why so few of the novels we have seen on the stage during the last few years have made plays of commensurate merit.

The man with a tale to tell has a choice of several ways in which to tell it. Some themes, no doubt, can only be satisfactorily handled in novel form, others are best as plays. But it is obvious that many themes are equally well adapted to either treatment. Many a novel contains the material for a good play; few good plays are made out of novels. It must logically follow that it is in faulty handling of the material that failure consists; and if so, there is no valid reason why such faults in handling should not be diagnosed and eradicated. The first part of the task—the diagnosis—is simple enough. These plays fail because they are bad plays; and they are bad plays because they are written not as plays but as dramatized novels, which is fatal. The adapter seems in almost every case to court disaster by writing with one eye—if not both—firmly fixed upon the novel from which he derived his first inspiration. In the book he comes across pieces of dialogue which please him—somehow they must be brought into the play; he finds scenes which make him laugh or cry—somehow a place must be found for these, too. Dialogue and scenes may all be quite extraneous to the main scheme of the novel, quite out of place in the more closely constructed fabric of a play; but the author has not the heart or the courage to make the necessary sacrifice. He alters his plot so as to drag in the passages in question "by the hair," and spoils his play. The most glaring example of this particular blunder that I can recall occurred in the stage version which Mr. Ian Hay made of his own novel, *The Safety Match*. There was in the book a very successful scene, in which two mischievous children, lunching by themselves at a big London restaurant, had a complicated passage-at-arms with a solemn but (as it turned out) far from unresourceful waiter. In the play none of the acts could be set in a restaurant; but the author could not bear to cut out this scene. He set to work with some ingenuity to invent a set of circumstances which would enable that particular incident to happen plausibly in a private house; but all the ingenuity in the world could not make it an integral part of the play. It became a little interlude, which held up the action of the play completely for fifteen minutes or so; and even then it proved not to be half so funny on the stage as in the book. In fact, it fell rather flat. A sad story—but I am not going to pretend that I don't think it served the author right.

This is just one example of the kind of thing which ruins the majority of adaptations. I am myself quite convinced that the proper way to adapt a novel for the stage, whether your own or another's, would be to read it through to get an idea of its main theme and its characters, and then to shut the book and get to work on an entirely independent dramatic composition—new in dialogue and, if necessary, in development. Only in this way could you be sure of resisting the temptation to include attractive but irrelevant material. Once the play was completed in the rough, you could turn back again to the book and use it to polish up such of your dialogue as had chanced to run on all-fours with that of the novel. I am quite aware that in many cases practical considerations would crop up to make the method that I have outlined extremely difficult to follow; but I am so far convinced of the rightness of the method as to assert dogmatically that you will not make good plays from novels by any other—except by accident.

In this connection novels fall naturally into two main categories—those by authors who are dead (which I will refer to loosely as "classics"), and those by living writers. If I am right in thinking that a novel can only be turned into a good play by a process of complete remoulding, it stands to reason that the adapters of "classics" are at a very great disadvantage. The best man—the only ideal man—to adapt a novel is its author; if lack of inclination or stage sense prevents him from doing the work, he should at least collaborate in it, should suggest alterations or additions and supervise their carrying out, and so preserve the unity of the conception. In the case of a "classic" an adapter has not the author's invention to rely upon, and is usually prevented by respect for his original, or fear of public opinion, from using his own. In consequence, I believe that the best that any man who sets out to adapt a "classic" can hope to achieve is honourable failure.[1]

Consider the difficulties that faced Mr. and Mrs. J. C. Squire when they decided to dramatize *Pride and Prejudice*. They held, perhaps, with Mr. A. B. Walkley, that Jane Austen's dialogue and her exquisite sense of character are essentially dramatic gifts, and that if she had been born into a more broad-minded generation she would probably (instead of making Fanny Price shudder at the mere mention of the word "theatricals") have chosen the stage as her means of expression. They determined to try to make out of *Pride and Prejudice* the play that it might have been. The book might be said to contain all the necessary material; their task was simply to take the book to pieces, select the bits they wanted, and rearrange them in a new pattern suitable for the stage. This is the strict and reverential method of adaptation—to admit no word or turn of phrase into the play that has not the authority of the original behind it. It is the natural method to use when handling work of such quality and delicacy as Jane Austen's, but it ties the adapter's hands intolerably. In fact, to speak brutally, it degrades him from the high calling of dramatist and makes of him some-

[1] The worst that he can achieve I know by sad experience to be almost incredibly bad. A recently seen version of Disraeli's *Tancred* may serve as an example.

thing more akin to the expert solver of jig-saw puzzles.

Unfortunately, if you are led to treat a work of art like a jig-saw it will behave as such. When you have taken a puzzle picture to bits you can put it together again to make only one satisfactory pattern—the original one. You cannot reject some of the pieces and make a new picture with the remainder; either there will be unsightly gaps in the new picture, or important bits will turn up that cannot be induced to fit in except by a drastic whittling down process that deprives them of all significance. Something of this kind happened in *Pride and Prejudice*. The dialogue retained the correct Austen flavour, but the characters seemed to dwindle away. Mr. and Mrs. Squire's version was received with the respect due to a gallant attempt, but all the same it brought upon itself stern disapproval from Mr. Walkley in his dual capacity of dramatic critic and Austen authority. For myself, I felt after this performance that what the authors had set out to do could hardly have been better done, and therefore could not have been successfully done at all.

So much for the strict method. Next in order come up for discussion those adaptations of "classics" whose makers, while sticking to their originals as closely as possible, have boldly invented new dialogue or incidents when nothing exactly suitable was to be found in the texts. Here the adapter stands to the playwright in much the same relationship as the skilled "faker" of old furniture stands to such artists as Chippendale or Sheraton. His task bristles with difficulties. If his "faking" is done with the least degree of clumsiness it becomes obvious to the most casual eye, and even at its most skilful it cannot hope to deceive the expert. In this connection I can produce a small piece of first-hand evidence. A short time ago I, in company with several other dramatic critics, went down to Dorchester to see the local players in their own dramatized version of Mr. Hardy's novel *Desperate Remedies.* I arrived in the town rather earlier than was strictly necessary, and during the afternoon I made the acquaintance of Alderman Tilley, the adapter. From him I learnt that Hardy himself takes practically no part in the preparation of his books for the local stage, beyond preserving a genial air of benevolence towards the players and their works. I at once asked Mr. Tilley whether he had found it possible to stick entirely to the original text, and he admitted that here and there he had found it necessary to interpolate incidents or dialogue of his own. He gave me one example—a scene which he considered (rightly, to my mind) would have "petered out" completely on the stage if presented as it stands in the book, and for which accordingly he had invented a more intense ending. A couple of hours later the curtain fell on that particular scene, and my neighbour—a fellow-critic who, having arrived by the later train, possessed no inside information—turned to me. "Well," said he, "I've never read *Desperate Remedies,* but I don't mind betting that Hardy never wrote that last bit of melodrama." Alderman Tilley does not, of course, claim to be anything more than an amateur author; his Hardy adaptations are a labour of love, a hobby for the spare moments of a busy life. It is probable that in his place a professional dramatist of experience would have succeeded in inventing for the scene in question an ending that would have been less obviously a "fake" and still have had the necessary dramatic "punch." But it does seem to me that even at the best you cannot expect by such a patchwork method to get a play fit to be compared, as a work of art, with the book from which it is taken. The highest hope of technical success in an adaptation of this kind is to be found where the adapter—being a dramatist of proved skill—has the courage to assert some measure of independence and put into his play so much of his own work that the "faking" metaphor ceases to apply to him. Of such a man it is fairer to say that he has taken his "classic" and boldly used it to supply specifications, foundation, and scaffolding whereby to erect in his own materials a building conforming to the original architect's design. The most successful example of this type that I have yet come across is Mr. J. B. Fagan's *Treasure Island*. In this case the adapter was favoured by his subject; he could not have followed the strict method if he had wanted to. There is hardly any actual talk in Stevenson's story, and therefore nearly all of the dialogue of the play is—because it must be—Mr. Fagan's own. It all sounds amazingly satisfactory on the stage.[1] And yet even here the classic proves intractable in the end. For all its fine rendering of the characters and atmosphere of

[1] It is interesting to notice that the one or two unconvincing details are supplied by such purely Stevensonian touches as Ben Gunn's curious idiom, which the adapter naturally felt himself bound to transfer direct from page to stage.

the book, for all its very solid commercial success and its annual revival, *Treasure Island* is not a good play. That is to say, it is not so good a play as it would have been if Mr. Fagan had felt himself as free to invent new incidents as he was to invent new dialogue. In this respect he was firmly shackled to the fame of his classic. If he had altered the plot a storm of protest would have broken over his head. We all know the story of *Treasure Island,* and we go to the theatre to see the story that is in the book, as near as may be. Stevenson, by taking full advantage of the novelist's privilege of mystifying his readers whenever he likes, keeps the secret of Benn Gunn's removal of the treasure, and so nurses the excitement of his book till the last pages. Mr. Fagan, compelled to give away this secret early in his play in order to make its development intelligible, is forced to a conclusion which is not a *dénouement* at all, but a sheer anti-climax.

This brings me to my second main category of adaptations—the books of living authors. I realize that if I am to make this a truly well-balanced essay I have at this point a plain duty to perform. Having established to my own satisfaction the inherent inadequacy of stage versions of classics and the reasons therefor, obviously I ought now to proceed to exhibit the bright side of the picture, to demonstrate by hosts of examples how comparatively easy contemporary writers find it to turn—or help to turn—their own books into good plays. But, alas, the truth must come before niceties of antithesis, and I have to confess my case is not so simple as all that. Two strong pieces of evidence are ready to hand, it is true. *The Little Minister* and *The Great Adventure* are good plays, because Barrie and Bennett, being playwrights as well as novelists, *did* construct their work anew when they prepared it for the stage; but beside these two[1] I can call to mind only a few pieces of successful work on a lower literary plane, of which *Tilly of Bloomsbury* and *Bulldog Drummond* are about the best. In both these cases the adapters brought considerable skill and judgment to the task of cutting away the unsuitable and selecting and supplementing the suitable parts of their novels.

When it comes to the production of negative evidence, however, I am in no difficulty. I can think of only too many adaptations which came to grief because they were not plays but mere paraphrases of the novels upon which they were based. It is, therefore, by the examination of some of these examples of " how not to do it " that I must hope to prove my point.

The great majority of the books which are turned into plays are novels with a wide popular appeal—the best-sellers. I have already made passing allusion to the peculiar difficulties and temptations which beset the man who sets out to adapt a work of this class. The chief consideration that leads to the dramatization of a " best-seller " is commercial.

[1] It is possible that *Kipps* ought to be added to the list. Unfortunately, when I saw it in 1912, no happy presentiment warned me to take mental notes in case I might some day want to compare its technique with that of other adaptations. Consequently, I remember little about it except the acting of Mr. O. B. Clarence and Miss Christine Silver, together with the fact that I considered at the time that my half-crown had been well spent.

The stage version is made, not because the novel in question is specially fitted for adaptation and is likely to make a good play, but simply because the public, having paid a great deal of money to enjoy the story in one form, may naturally be expected to pay still more to enjoy it in another. This commercial consideration dictates the very form that the stage version is to take, making a "best-seller" just as difficult to adapt as a classic. Indeed a "best-seller" may be defined with fair accuracy as a temporary classic, for during the period of its vogue it holds among undiscriminating readers just that position of honour which people of more sophisticated taste reserve for genuine classics. Consequently, the pressure of public interest compels the adapter to confine himself to translating the book with reasonable efficiency and as literally as may be into terms of the stage. Sometimes, in the case of novelists of the Ethel M. Dell or Gertrude Page order, stage versions thus made turn out commercial successes; more often they fail, being (like most translations) halting and unsatisfactory pieces of work. Miss Dell's *The Way of an Eagle* was a fair, and Miss Page's *Paddy the Next Best Thing* a great, popular success in the theatre; the same two authors' *Knave of Diamonds* and *Edge o' Beyond* were almost failures. None of these four plays established a claim to be judged by any but a low critical standard, and the success of one or failure of another seems to me to have depended less upon the comparative merits of the plays than upon the comparative popularity of the players. Paddy introduced Miss Peggy O'Neil to an adoring public in a tomboy part which just suited her unmistakable talents and rather overwhelming personality, while the opportunity of seeing Mr. Godfrey Tearle as the Dellian Strong Man must have been a bait that few flappers could resist. In order, therefore, to put the case for the adapted "best-seller" in as favourable an artistic light as possible, I will take as my example that most pronounced of all popular favourites—Mr. A. S. M. Hutchinson's *If Winter Comes*.

This novel was the work of a serious literary artist whose aim is to understand and portray human nature, not to caricature it after the ecstatic manner of the Ethel M. Dells of this world. The miraculous success of the book made the eventual appearance of a stage version a foregone conclusion, quite irrespective of the suitability or otherwise of the story for this purpose; and the narrative style of Mr. Hutchinson is so diffuse, his method of development so leisurely, as to be quite unfitted for the stage. So far the omens concerning Mr. Basil Macdonald Hastings' adaptation could not be called good. But still there did seem to be a chance that so experienced a dramatist, given the theme and characters, might be able to make a good play out of *If Winter Comes* by allowing his dramatic story to develop naturally along its own lines. But when Mr. Hastings got to work he found himself forced by the presumed weight of public opinion to make a mere *pis aller*—a version ingeniously manipulated so as to contain not only theme and characters, but as many of the incidents of the book as possible. The result was a play so episodic that playgoers who had not read the book found themselves at a loss to comprehend motives which had been completely clear in the original, which is to say that a great part of the human understanding to which Mr. Hutchinson owed his immense popularity had evaporated in the process of adaptation.

Thus we come to the last and best class of all, to which *The Little Minister, The Great Adventure, Kipps, Tilly of Bloomsbury* and *Bulldog Drummond* can all be assigned—the books which are selected for adaptation in the first instance because their authors discern in them the makings of a play. Sometimes the authors are wrong, because human judgment (in all things fallible) is in no one respect less reliable than in matters concerning the theatre. Accordingly, this class contains, besides its few successful ventures, a number that were foredoomed from the outset to failure. The swift death of Mr. H. G. Wells's *The Wonderful Visit* was due rather to an inherent unsuitability of its subject to the stage, coupled with an unsuccessful experiment in production, than to any shortcomings on the part of Mr. St. John Ervine, the adapter. But even in cases where the author's choice of a theme is justified, the results of his labours are too often disappointing. This brings me to the saddest and the most convincing of all my cautionary examples—the failure of Joseph Conrad's own stage version of his novel *The Secret Agent*. I am sure that the story of this book does lend itself to dramatic treatment, that there was a good play to be made out of it. I am still more certain that Conrad did not make it. His version as produced at the Ambassadors Theatre was not a commercial failure only (as certain disgruntled literary men would have us believe), but a dramatic failure too. *The Secret Agent* failed because it was a bad play; and it was a bad play because its author did not take his novel to pieces and reconstruct it before beginning to rewrite.

An immediate result of that failure was a perfect howl of execration and recrimination, such as is always raised over the failure on the stage of any play whose claims to respect are more literary than dramatic. As usual, the dramatic critics were saddled with the chief share of the blame; they were held up to derision as a set of ignorant vandals, who, while spending their time crying out for something better in the theatre, could not recognize that something better when they got it, and dared to flout genius when it condescended to their base level. This is the invariable attitude of a certain type of "literary" mind to the theatre, and it is obviously a provocative attitude, leading to heated argument rather than to calm judgment. "Can't you understand," asks the literary critic, with galling superiority, "that Conrad is a genius who ought to be safe from the attacks of a miserable pipsqueak like you?" "If he's a genius," retorts the pipsqueak fiercely, "why did he write such a damned bad play?" In the dust of the ensuing mêlée the main question is lost sight of, and the cause of literature in the theatre suffers.

That the failure of the play was a real calamity to the theatre I have no doubt at all. Our stage has long been handicapped by the fact that few of our best writers appear to consider it worthy of their attention.[1] Presumably they resent its limited technique, its comparatively rigid form. A novel may be written in any shape the fancy of its author may dictate; its story may be told (as readers of Conrad have every reason to know) as brilliantly upside-down as right way up, but a play is less accommodating. If *The Secret Agent* had been a good play, it would have been a powerful weapon with which to break down that prejudice; but its failure only adds another and massive stone to the fabric. Where Conrad failed, other novelists of Conrad's magnitude will be less inclined to venture; but indeed, where Conrad failed they are only too certain to fail too, unless they adapt themselves better than he did to a less malleable medium than the novel.

In writing his adaptation Conrad seemed to have forgotten the theatre altogether. Unconsciously he aimed at making nothing more than a translation of his novel into stage idiom. He broke up his narrative into acts and scenes, he told his story by means of dialogue, and he arranged his dialogue within those acts and scenes in such a way that an audience could arrive at the end of a performance with a complete knowledge of the main incidents and characters of his novel, *The Secret Agent*. But he did not write a play. Hardly once did his dialogue give the

[1] Mr. Galsworthy is the brilliant exception, for he writes plays fit to rank beside his novels; and he studies the requirements of the stage, as he has himself made clear in his preface to Conrad's *Laughing Anne* and *One Day More*. Mr. Arnold Bennett, on the other hand, often seems to write for the theatre as though he despised it. As a result, not only has he never written a play fit to be mentioned in the same breath with *The Old Wives' Tale*, but he has had a whole series of dismal and uncompromising failures in the theatre.

impression of being intended to be spoken rather than read. Never but in the last scenes did he rely upon action to such an extent as to suggest that his appeal was addressed to the eye as well as to the ear.

An example may be found in the handling of the incident upon which the whole plot turns—that point in the story where Verloc, the *agent provocateur,* bidden by the secret service that employs him to commit an outrage which will result in a wholesale arrest of anarchists by the British police, works upon the impressionable mind of his half-witted young brother-in-law, Stevie, and excites him into such a state that he consents to bomb the Observatory at Greenwich. The boy manages to blow himself to pieces instead, and Mrs. Verloc, finding out what has happened, kills her husband and goes mad.

Now, by allowing the bomb episode to take place in an interval between acts, Conrad uses in his dramatization the methods of the novelist; more, he commits the novelist's commonest and most fatal stage crime. By the end of the first act we know that Verloc is to blow up the Observatory, and we have something more than an inkling that Stevie is to play an important part in that operation. We look forward, naturally, to finding out what that part is to be; but by the time the curtain rises on the next act the explosion has already happened. Gradually we are allowed to apprehend details—at first vaguely, through a bare report in an evening paper and a discussion held thereon by one or two of the genuine anarchists; afterwards more exactly, by means of a conversation between crime experts at Scotland Yard. Bit by bit it appears that something has gone wrong with Verloc's scheme—that the bomb has exploded not at the Observatory but in an open place in Greenwich Park; that a man has been blown to pieces; and finally that Stevie is the victim. Later still we hear the story from Verloc's own lips, and realize that Stevie's death was no fault of his, but an accident which he could not prevent. From the novelist's point of view this method of development is beautifully thought out and delicately adjusted; but it is quite undramatic.

For stage purposes the one essential thing here should have been to let the audience know for certain, and at once, exactly what Verloc's intentions were, what part he had assigned to Stevie, and how the plan came to grief. That is to say, it was Conrad's plain duty as dramatist to give us a scene in Greenwich Park just before the accident. The material for such a scene is all outlined in the conversation between Verloc and Inspector Heat, which comes in the middle of the last act as the play stands:

HEAT: I would have roped in half a dozen of your fellows over this affair if I had been left alone. I don't mean you. I have known you too long. You meant no harm.

VERLOC: Look here! The boy was half an idiot. If he had been caught it would have been the asylum for him, nothing worse. I told him what to do twenty times over. Made him repeat it all that morning. Then I left him and went away to wait until he had done it. It was foggy early this morning. We could have both got clear. I was waiting for him.

HEAT: The bang startled you, eh? Came too soon?

VERLOC: Yes, it came too soon. I knew then that he was gone, and I ran down Chesterfield Walk. I don't think I met anyone till I was past the end of George Street.

HEAT : So easy as that! We think he stumbled against a tree root, you know. . . .

This scene is necessary to the play as it stands, for it is after she has overheard it that Winnie Verloc stabs her husband. But if it had also been translated into action at the beginning of the second act; if we had heard Verloc giving Stevie his instructions and making him repeat them, had seen the boy set out with the bomb while Verloc waited, and had heard in the distance the bang which came too soon, we should then have sat up and asked ourselves the real questions of the play—Will Winnie learn what we already know? And, if so, how will she act?

But Conrad, who had rightly avoided direct description of this scene in his book, failed to realize that a method which is exactly right for a novel is often exactly wrong for a play; and as a result the stage was the chief loser.

I have tried to make this little survey as comprehensive as possible, but I have not been able within the confines of one short article to examine all the available evidence. The list of plays from which I have picked my examples—a list made and added to at random, but as complete as my memory can supply—contains thirty titles. It may be, however, that some stubborn soul requires still more weight of testimony to convince him than an adapter, to get the best results, must be prepared boldly to reject attractive but unnecessary material, and equally boldly to invent new material where it is needed. For him, if he exists, I have one good shot left in the locker. I refer him to the works of Shakespeare, *passim*.

ACADEMIC CRITICISM

WHEN I published my earlier volume of essays on the theatre, I found myself very severely taken to task by Mr. Gilbert Norwood, who happens to be not only a gifted writer, but also Professor of Greek in the University College of South Wales at Cardiff. His chief complaint against me was that I had given more space in my book to Mr. John Drinkwater's *Abraham Lincoln* than to Miss Clemence Dane's *Will Shakespeare.* Mr. Norwood had himself no very high opinion of the former play, and considered the latter to be "beyond comparison the greatest and most beautiful play of our time." Finding in my book no statement of a corresponding enthusiasm, he accused me of saying that I liked *Lincoln* merely because the fashion of the hour so dictated, and of paying less attention to *Will Shakespeare* because I could not recognize beautiful and noble work when I saw it.

As it happened, my critic's whole accusation was founded on a misunderstanding of the scope and nature of my book. He criticized *Through the Fourth Wall* as though it had set out to be a comprehensive survey of the contemporary theatre; whereas it was, like this present volume,[1] nothing

[1] It may be as well to remark here that although none of the essays in this book happens to be about *St. Joan,* it should not therefore be assumed that I am blind to the quality of Mr. Shaw's finest play.

more ambitious than a random collection of papers contributed from time to time to the periodical Press, and dealing with whatever subjects happened to be uppermost in my mind at the time when I had leisure to write them. In point of fact, during the period covered by those essays I had written at considerable length about Miss Dane's play, besides having a private correspondence on the subject with its producer; but as my articles on *Will Shakespeare* had all, through force of circumstances, been hastily written for immediate publication, I could not, in justice to my readers, have reprinted them.

However, this is by the way. I do not propose to shelter myself behind Mr. Norwood's mistake, nor to evade his criticism, for he has arrived accidentally at a perfectly correct conclusion. I *do* consider *Abraham Lincoln* a better play than *Will Shakespeare*—not because " the fashion of the hour so dictates," but because I judge the two plays as a dramatic critic while Mr. Norwood (though I have good reason to believe him to be the least donnish of professors) brings to bear upon them the academic mind. The fundamental quarrel between us is, not that he has standards of criticism while I have none, but that each of us has standards which the other does not recognize—or, at any rate, does not respect.

You could hardly have a better instance to prove once again how deep and wide is the divergence between the two kinds of critics of the drama—those who judge plays on the stage and those who deal with them chiefly in the study. To Mr. Norwood, in his armchair, revelling in the beauty of the language and the imagery in Miss Dane's play, *Will Shakespeare* was beyond comparison the greatest and most beautiful play of our time; to me, in my stall, it was nothing more than a brilliant failure. I saw it three times, and its effect on me varied hardly a hair's-breadth. After each hearing I went home oppressed with the same feeling of sadness, that the play had so nearly achieved, and had yet so definitely fallen short of, greatness. As it happens, one day recently I read somewhere a passage in which this play was spoken of as "a masterpiece in the study and a travesty on the stage." That is putting the two aspects of the play in startling contrast of black and white; but it defines the issue. Now, to my way of thinking, no man is justified in describing any composition as "a great play" unless it has proved great in action on the stage. *Will Shakespeare* did not prove so. If my critic had called it "a great dramatic poem," or something else of the sort designed to show that he was considering its merits as a piece of literature, without much reference to stage-craft, it would have been another matter entirely. But he did not. He left no door open to appeal. He simply stated, as a fact, that *Will Shakespeare* is "beyond comparison the greatest play of our time," and left an unmistakable inference to be drawn that anybody who disagreed with him was without judgment or standards.

To my mind, he is here talking through his professorial mortar-board. That *Will Shakespeare* is a fine literary achievement few will be found to deny; that it is a great play is not proven, and, as I think, never will be proven. Miss Dane seems to me to have ruined her play's chance of being great in action by one or two fundamental errors. The first, and less important, of these is faulty stage-craft. I have always maintained that the long and dramatically ineffective "vision scene" ought to have been cut clean out of the play, and that the play would have been a very much better stage composition after such an operation. The second, and immeasurably worse, fault is the unimpressive manner in which the central figure is drawn.

Before I could accept Miss Dane's hero as the authentic Shakespeare, I should have to be converted to a belief that the plays were written by Bacon, or Oxford, or Queen Elizabeth, or whom you will. The Will Shakespeare of the play is a mere nobody. He exhibits not even the germs of greatness. He is entirely lacking in that rich understanding of humanity which the author of the great comedies must have possessed. A pretty, superficial tragedy is about his literary mark, and he could as easily have translated the Koran as have written *Hamlet*. Funnily enough, in the same year which saw *Will Shakespeare* run its course, another play on the same theme saw the light. This was *Shakespeare*, by Messrs. Clifford Bax and H. F. Rubinstein; I saw it acted (very poorly for the most part) at a special Sunday night performance at the Court Theatre. Nobody has been found to hail this play as the greatest of our time, or even to venture on producing it for a run. But I find the Shakespeare of that play "beyond comparison" the more convincing of the two as a portrait of the man who wrote the plays. And bad as the conditions were under which I saw it acted, I thought this part gave Mr. Ion Swinley better chances for fine acting than Mr. Philip Merivale could find in Miss Dane's more famous version.

I have no desire to labour the argument as between Mr. Norwood and me; but I do think it important to state a case against academic criticism of plays, because it is largely to such criticism that our theatre owes its present inability to appeal to a highly educated public. Whenever a literary man publishes a play which is finely written, the academic critics hail it as a dramatic masterpiece. If it is then tried in the theatre and proves a dramatic failure, its non-success is regarded by the academic critics as a reflection, not on their judgment but on the theatre and everything connected with it. The educated public, having in its turn read the play but not seen it, agrees to despise the theatre; and the writers who wish to appeal to that public either ignore the theatre altogether, or write for it without having studied its special requirements. And thus the vicious circle is completed.

America has the same problem to face. Mr. Clayton Hamilton, one of the best of the American dramatic critics, dealt with the point in his book *Problems of the Playwright,* published in 1917. He begins:

Brander Matthews, not many years ago, in reviewing a book by the Professor of English Literature in the University of Leeds, defined it as an essay in "undramatic criticism." The author of that academic volume had persistently regarded the drama as something to be read, instead of regarding it as something devised to be represented by actors on a stage before an audience. His criticism, therefore, took no account of the conditions precedent to any valid exercise of the art that he was criticizing.

The contemporary drama suffers more than that of any other period from the comments of "undramatic critics" who know nothing of the exigencies of the theatre. In the first place, the contemporary drama is more visual in its appeal than the drama of the past, and what it says to the eye can hardly be recorded adequately on the printed page. In the second place, the rapid evolution of the modern art of stage direction has made the drama more and more, in recent years, unprintable. And, in the third place, the contemporary drama, with its full and free discussion of topics that are current in the public mind, requires—more than that of any other period—the immediate collaboration of a gathered audience. Such a drama can be judged with fairness only in the theatre, for which it was devised.

The fallacy of "undramatic criticism" of contemporary drama is a fallacy to which professors in our universities are particularly prone. The reason is not far to seek. The prison-house of their profession confines them, for the most part, to little towns and little cities where no theatre, that is worthy of the name, exists. Condemned to see nothing of the current theatre, they are driven back to the library, to cull their knowledge of the modern drama from the dubious records of the printed page.

Having said so much, Mr. Hamilton proceeds to examine three cases in point, being books on contemporary drama, each by a professor in an American university. These are *Modern Drama,* by Lewisohn, of Ohio; *Aspects of Modern Drama,* by Chandler, of Cincinnati; and *The Changing Drama,* by Henderson, of North Carolina. Not once, in any one of the three big books supposed to deal exhaustively with the playwrights of to-day, is there any mention of J. M. Barrie. At the time when Mr. Hamilton was writing Barrie's plays had not been published, whence he concludes, and backs his argument by much convincing evidence, that " in academic books about the modern drama the ranking of the living British dramatists is proportioned directly in accordance to the pompousness with which their plays have been printed and bound and published to the reading world."

The whole case against the professors is summed up in that phrase, " undramatic critics " of Brander Matthews (himself a very famous and distinguished professor, so that the indictment comes from a quarter in which it cannot easily be met). Personally, I cannot understand how anybody can dream of judging whether a play is " great " or not without having seen it acted. The general consensus of opinion of all the producers and actors with whom I have ever discussed the question is that you never can tell in any exact degree what a play is like merely from reading the text. My own experience confirms this. My last year at Cambridge was entirely devoted to an intensive course of " undramatic criticism " of English drama—especially Shakespeare. During that year I read everything that Shakespeare had written or might have written, together with a most unconscionable amount of matter which had been written about him. At the end of the year I was crammed with knowledge about Shakespeare the dramatic poet, Shakespeare the literary genius, the sonnet-writer, the prosodist, the actor, the Stratford burgess, the " ghost " of Bacon, and so on. But if I went to see any of the plays that year—which I doubt—I went entirely in the spirit of a man about to pass a stiff Shakespeare examination. The result was that Shakespeare the playwright (who is the Shakespeare that matters most) never dawned on my consciousness till later, when I went to the theatre again as a free man. I quote this chapter in my past as a warrant for stating my firm view that the "undramatic" critic is in no position to judge anything but the literary value of a play. If he decides that a composition is a great piece of literature, he ought not to pronounce it a great play until he has been to the theatre to discover whether it is a play at all.

OBER-AMMERGAU

I

When I set out for Ober-Ammergau I had never been in Germany, and—except for one or two unsociable meetings during the war—had never encountered the Teuton in bulk. I was in consequence at least as interested in the prospect of seeing Germany in general as of witnessing the Passion Play in particular. My travelling companion, who had known Munich before the war, was rather excited at the prospect of finding out what difference the war had made. But I was even more excited at the idea of finding out what sort of a country it was that had unloosed those five hectic years upon us. We left Calais soon after noon by the Orient express—the amazing train which takes Munich easily in its stride before continuing its course towards Vienna and, eventually, Bucharest. It is a spasmodic sort of train, really, because when it is not whirling you at immense speed through continents, it selects some totally unknown spot in which to spend an hour or two of silent meditation. Do you know a suburb of Paris called Gagny? No? Well, if I had only the Orient express to depend on, Gagny is the spot in France that I should know best. Not a bad little place in its way—but a little lacking in that abandon for which the Englishman is taught to look in Paris. In fact, a very decorous suburb, as seen from the train, inhabited by one dog and two small children.

It was dead of night when we reached Nancy, and my next recollection after that is of being awakened at the frontier to have my passport endorsed. The French official, having had his go at the document, handed it over to his German opposite number, who was so exactly like the German officer of the English comic papers that I—half-awake as I was—felt that I could not really be awake at all. I was in Germany a week, but I did not see another German half so typical as this one. Perhaps they keep him on the frontier on purpose, as a kind of sample specimen.

Next time I woke we were well inside Germany, and I began to take stock of my impressions as a good tourist should. My companion had made the journey several times before, and began picking out remembered landmarks—it was all familiar ground to him. But after a little a feeling began to grow in my mind that it was somehow familiar to me, too. I had seen it all before somewhere—or something just like it. But where? Not in this life, certainly; and so I found myself combating the dismal alternative that I had either been a German myself in a previous existence or had now found, like Lord Haldane, my spiritual home. We passed through a wayside town, more inexplicably familiar than ever, and I was really becoming quite distressed over it, when we happened to pass a specimen of the strange type of open-work railway signal which the German affects; and my little problem was solved. That signal took me back in imagination to my nursery floor, where I played happily with a model railway just given me by an indulgent parent.

When I was at the model-railway age small boys were not the sticklers for realism that they are now, and the name of Bassett-Lowke would have failed to stir my infant heart to a quicker beat. But even so, I remember that I found the shape of my locomotive and its coaches unsatisfactorily unlike anything I had travelled in or behind; I found the stations with which Gamage's catalogue confronted me quite different from my idea of a station; and when somebody gave me an open-work signal I simply refused to play with the thing. . . . We passed through another town, and this time I realized why the architecture also struck so responsive a chord. My finest toy in that same nursery had been a wonderful series of boxes of stone bricks, complete with building plans and elevations, with which I had spent happy hours building strangely un-English churches and bridges and town halls—of which I was now, for the first time, gazing upon the originals. Never before had I realized how deep an impression those old playthings, all marked "Made in Germany," had made on me. But I was relieved to be able to drop the reincarnation theory.

We arrived in Munich soon after mid-day on Sunday in brilliant sunshine. My companion suggested that we should spend the afternoon in exploring the town, and go on to Ober-Ammergau by the late train. I naturally fell in with this scheme; but before doing anything else whatever we determined to have a meal. Accordingly, feeling in a mood to do ourselves proud, we sought out the best hotel in the place, ate an excellent lunch, washed it down with an equally excellent bottle of wine, and called for the bill. After all that we had been told of the cheapness of living in Germany at the then rate of exchange, neither of us had expected to be rendered exactly penniless by this meal; but both of us were staggered when, after working the formidable total of marks with which we were presented back into English currency, I found that the sum demanded of each of us was two and fourpence. When I got back to London my friends accused me of being a soulless clod because I talked more about the price of food and less about the Passion Play than they thought right or seemly. But my answer was that there were many points about the Passion Play which, as a dramatic critic, I should have liked to have seen done otherwise; while in my private capacity as a poor man who is no expert in economics I had nothing but praise for a system which enabled you for sixpence-halfpenny to feast (as we feasted that evening at a beerhall) on an omelette the size of a young bolster and a flagon of beer that could not have held much under a quart. Indeed, by the time I left Germany the excellence of this jest of fortune had not even begun to wear off. I felt all the time like a man who has suddenly come into an unexpected fortune, half afraid that I might wake up and find the whole thing a fantastic dream and myself penniless through unduly riotous living. Before I leave this sordid subject I must put on record, since those fortunate days have passed never to return, the most striking of all the prices I came across; and as it happens it has nothing to do with food. A berth in the sleeping-car from Munich to Frankfort (nine hours of my return journey) cost tenpence.

We spent that afternoon in Munich, wondering at the air of gay and irresponsible prosperity that pervaded the place, sitting in the park which overlooks the Iser, and later in the gardens of the now disused Royal palace. Then, having consumed our bolsters as aforesaid, we left by the last train for Ober-Ammergau. This journey was one of the slowest in my experience (and I have lived in Wales); it took us four and a half hours to cover about fifty miles. But I could not regret it. The Orient express is a lordly means of locomotion, but it does not give you much leisure to observe the life of the country. This train did; and on a Sunday night in Bavaria there is plenty of life to observe. Our train was full of merry peasants in the picturesque national dress (themselves also full of the national beverage) going home after a day in Munich. In the other direction came trainloads of equally merry Muncheners, coming home after indulgence in the long country walks which seem to be the Bavarian's chief form of exercise. There was a good deal of singing going on; and on the platform of one wayside station a brass band was in full blast, whiling away the time till its train arrived. Soon it did arrive, and the band ceased fire, scrambled aboard and put away its instruments—all but the trombonist. That enthusiast was to be seen in a fourth-class carriage gaily carrying on his part of the entertainment as a solo, oblivious of the fact that his instrument, both in shape and manner of manipulation, is quite the worst suited of all to be played in such a place. What were the feelings of his vis-à-vis is unfortunately not in my power to record.

It was nearly midnight when we alighted from the little electric railway which toils from Murnau into the Ober-Ammergau uplands. The bright moonlight gave us little more than a vague impression of hills and houses. The first sign that we were now really arrived on the scene of the Passion Play was the sight of several minor apostles and a Pharisee or two, all with long hair, among the small crowd which met the train at the station. Next day the village and its surroundings turned out to be a kind of little Switzerland. From my window Ober-Ammergau was visible as a tangle of blue and red and grey roofs, on which the sun was shining with great strength. On the steep pine-covered mountains which encircle the place on every side snow was still lying as a reminder of recent bad weather. At that time (I am speaking of early May, before the first public performance of the Passion Play was given) there were few visitors in the place, and the queer little winding streets, which seem to slip in and out between the houses by accident, were not more busy than you would expect of any other village of the size. But on every side the sound of saw and hammer rose to heaven, showing where the inhabitants were feverishly at work renovating their houses and building new ones (including an impressive hotel with an American bar) ready for the expected influx of tourists.

When I went out and began to poke about, the village revealed itself still further as a real study in contrasts. You might encounter country carts drawn by oxen—in fact, I saw one in which an ox and a horse were yoked together and acting in perfect unity—side by side with which you might see an up-to-date motor-bus plying between Ober-Ammergau and the neighbouring town of Garmisch, which stands just on the Austrian border, and is the home of Richard Strauss. Anton Lang (the famous Christus of the play) at work in his pottery shop looked like a patriarch out of the Old Testament; yet the front of that same shop proudly displays beneath his name—his telephone number! Every house in the village has electric light, but the fact that there is in the place one private house fitted with a bath is a fact of enough public interest to be noted in the guide-books.

On that first day of my sojourn, nothing of importance was being done about the Passion Play itself. On the previous day had been held the first of all the series of performances—the private dress rehearsal, to which no strangers are admitted, and to which the inhabitants of the neighbourhood are invited free of charge. On the morrow the public dress rehearsal for the Press was to take place. In the meantime, the actors were carrying on with their ordinary work, and the chief event of the day was a parade of the local fire brigade, to which some of the actors belong. A brass helmet perched on the top of a long biblical coiffure produces a romantic Joan of Arc effect which you can imagine better than I can describe. But however easily the fire brigade may move frivolous-minded people like myself to laughter, I imagine it is not the least necessary institution in this village. For most of the houses are of wood, built to that châlet pattern which took me back as irresistibly as the open-work signals to my nursery floor and the door of my long-forgotten toy-cupboard.

II

I am not yet certain whether I saw the Passion Play from the best or the worst possible part of the theatre. On the whole, I am inclined to think the best. Certainly that was the intention of the Burgomaster and the Committee who had invited us all to the special Press Rehearsal, and had provided us with the much sought-after first-class seats. There are no galleries in the Ober-Ammergau Theatre; its four thousand seats are arranged on one sloping floor, and at the very back are the boxes where tremendous personages sit when such happen to be present. Just in front of these boxes, and in the centre of the house, were the seats allotted to us. When the play began I found that I was too far from the stage to be able to see the shades of expression on the faces of the actors, and too far away to follow the words unless I had (as we all had) a copy of the text open on my knees. But on the other hand, we were just far enough away from the enormous stage to be able to take in the whole of its sweep at one glance; and that, I have almost convinced myself after mature consideration, is the most important thing.

But there were times, particularly during the soliloquy scenes of Judas Iscariot, when from my aristocratic eminence I envied the humble groundlings in the distance.

Nor was I alone in this idea. There was a very charming American lady staying in our hotel. She was just an ordinary tourist, and consequently had no kind of right to be present at the Press Rehearsal at all; but no method has yet been invented by which charming American ladies can be hindered from doing anything and going anywhere they like, and so she had managed to "scrounge" from somewhere a fourth-class ticket. Even this triumph did not satisfy her; and at the last moment she managed, to her great joy, to exchange it for a returned press-ticket just behind ours. When we all reached the theatre, and found that our places were several miles from the stage, she strolled off to see where the despised fourth-class seats were, and liked them so much better that she decided to change again.

Accordingly, she reappeared in company with a picturesque peasant, whom she had bribed to take her seat for his own by offering him thirty times its market value. The peasant had had his wife with him, but sentiment was not proof against the lure of riches plus an opportunity to hobnob with the mighty. Just as he was taking his new seat, however, a new character arrived on the scene in the shape of a prosperous-looking German, who evidently considered himself aggrieved at having to sit in the fourth-class seats at all. This gentleman's idea was that the American lady, since her tastes were so unaccountably low, should have *his* seat; that the peasant should then return to his deserted spouse; and that he himself should sit in the first-class seat, where he belonged. The peasant, a little dazed, but still business-like, agreed to this—for a further consideration; and there followed an argument as to terms, at any moment of which I expected the authorities to eject the participants for unseemly brawling, and our enterprising American for incitement.

However, the storm died down at last; the peasant returned to his wife, bulging with unexpected wealth; and the lady changed seats with the last arrival. When the first part of the performance was over we met again for lunch, and it was obvious that she had seen far more of the acting than we had; but in spite of this, I am still inclined to think that the Passion Play is better seen from afar off.

After all, the thing that makes the Passion Play something more than an ordinary play—the thing that makes it worth travelling a thousand miles to see—is not the acting; at least, not the individual acting. Rather is it the general effect and atmosphere of the whole. If you were to go to Ober-Ammergau simply with the idea of witnessing a work of deliberate art you would, I think, be disappointed. Judged by a rigid standard of criticism the music is nothing out of the ordinary, and many of the costumes—particularly those of the chorus—reflect the least attractive period of religious painting. The singing is good—for a village; the technique of the acting is good—for a village. But if you refuse to make allowances, and expect a finished professional production, your thousand-mile pilgrimage will have been wasted. Some of the individual acting is astonishingly good, not merely "for a village"; many times did I regret my forgotten field-glasses, whose absence prevented me from watching more closely the details of the acting of Anton Lang himself, of Guido Mayr as Judas, of Paula Rendl as Mary Magdalene. But never for one moment could I forget that this spectacle was essentially a religious festival, and only incidentally a histrionic display. The moving force behind it—the thing which kept a huge audience silent and spell-bound on hard seats for eight hours, unmindful of cramped limbs and aching bones—was the force of tradition rather than dramatic virtuosity, of emotion rather than judgment, of religious awe rather than artistic appreciation.

(Even as I write these words, my mind misgives me; the dividing line between religion and art is so narrow and so easily crossed that I feel I am overbold to attempt to draw it so firmly. " Art," says Goethe, " rests upon a kind of religious sense; it is deeply and ineradicably in earnest." The distinction I want to draw is between works of art which are also incidentally works of religion (for example, *The Showing Up of Blanco Posnet*), and works of religion which happen to be also works of art; such as the Passion Play. The Passion Play, certainly, is a work of art, because it is a story in effective dramatic form, and conforms to Goethe's requirements by being deeply and ineradicably in earnest. But if it were purely, instead of only incidentally, a work of art, it would not be worth as much consideration as—well, as *Blanco Posnet*.)

Every child born in Ober-Ammergau is bred up in the tradition of the Passion Play; from the time that it begins to speak it looks forward to the time when it shall be one of the five or six hundred chosen to perform. In many families the tradition is handed down from generation to generation, so that the same names appear time and again in the records of the play. In 1922, for instance, the small part of Mark was taken by old Rochus Lang, father of Anton; Hans Mayr (Pilate) is son of Josef Mayr, the famous Christus of last century; Paula Rendl (Magdalene) is daughter of a former Herod. Steeped as they are in the spirit of the play, the villagers do not act the story so much as live it.

The effect of this is felt most in the crowd scenes. The very first scene of the play proper is Christ's triumphal entry into Jerusalem; and I was at once convinced that there never had been or could be such a crowd as this on any professional stage. So long as a stage crowd is small enough and compact enough, a producer of character can achieve wonderful results; but in any band of "supers" of really considerable size you will always be able to pick out one or two at least who are merely going perfunctorily through the movements they have been taught. Their minds are on other things. If they talk among themselves you feel sure they are speaking of the audience, of the three-thirty race—in fact, of anything in the world but the subject of the play in which they are supposed to be taking part. There were no weaker brethren of this kind in the Ober-Ammergau crowd—a crowd, moreover, of a size which could be accommodated by the stage of no ordinary theatre. Search that crowd as I might, I could not find a single member of it who was not deeply and whole-heartedly engrossed in the action that was going forward, from the palm-bearers round about Christ Himself down to the children that pushed and struggled on the crowd's outskirts to get a view somehow of what was happening. A tradition which is strong enough to produce such an all-embracing effect as this must, I believe, be religious rather than artistic.

I have insisted on this point at some length because upon it depends your whole attitude as a spectator of the Passion Play. As it happened, my travelling companion came to Ober-Ammergau expecting to see, first and foremost, a work of art; while I, as I have said, was strongly impressed from the first with its essentially religious character. The different effects the play had on each of us are instructive. He came away from the theatre at the end of the day disappointed, and aching with boredom, regarding the music with contempt, the play in general with indifference, and the scene on Calvary with actual revulsion; his first remark to me afterwards (when he could bring himself to speak at all) was that he now, for the first time, fully sympathized with the ancient Greeks in their determination not to allow any deed of violence or horror to be done actually on the stage. The Crucifixion scene had not affected me in that way at all. I had accepted it not at its dramatic worth as a terribly realistic representation of a shocking piece of barbarity, but at its religious value as a magnificent act of remembrance and worship.

III

Looking back on my visit to Ober-Ammergau, I recognize clearly enough that I was not impressed quite as I had hoped to be. My appreciation was a thing more of the intellect than of the imagination. So far as I at least am concerned, the inner glory of Ober-Ammergau has departed with the coming of that American bar and all that it stands for. To have come upon the Passion Play in the years before the village was discovered by Mr. Thomas Cook and his American equivalents must have been an adventure to remember with wonder all one's days. You can get—or at least, I could get—no such experience there now.

By virtue of its remoteness, and of the ten years that lie between one production of the Passion Play and another—years in which the thoughts of the Cook's tourist turn in other directions—the village has preserved its simplicity to a wonderful extent. But the modern improvements give a self-conscious, striving air to that simplicity; and after a while I began to feel an unwilling doubt whether, in any deep sense, it still existed. That doubt slipped away from me in the theatre, but returned in the hotel. I still believe it to be an unworthy thought; but I still cannot quite shake it off.

At any rate our charming American had no such doubts. She had travelled many a league in order to be impressed, and she *was* impressed, most completely and thoroughly. Having exhausted her vocabulary over the play, she next proceeded to discover in the village an artist of heaven-born genius. He was a wild-eyed child of nature in a blue blouse and a beard, whom she had found (I am not quite clear how) engaged in one of the lower walks of his profession—to wit, white-washing a house. She brought him and his sketches of the chief characters of the play along to the hotel for us to admire, and told us with bated breath how he was so full of temperament that the thought of suicide was never very far from his mind. She proposed that we should make known his powers to the world at large, and so win for ourselves a reflected glory. Unfortunately, the exhibition did not turn out to be so great a success as she had expected. The artist was indeed a clever draughtsman so far as he went; even to our limited knowledge that much was apparent. Indeed, our reception of his first picture was all that his patroness could desire; but as portrait succeeded portrait an extraordinary monotony of pose manifested itself. At last, my companion put a question which my few halting words of German could not compass, and the artist cheerfully admitted that he could only draw heads and hands—a form of specialism as cramping to the style as that of Lewis Carroll's baker, who could only bake bride-cake.

I am not sure that the lady ever quite forgave us because, after inspecting the masterpieces, we did not immediately rush to the post-office and set the telegraph-wires humming. I think she feared that disappointment would drive her protégé to that suicide of which he was accustomed to speak so freely. Any misgivings on that score that I may myself have entertained were set at rest next morning when, on my way to the station, I saw the man of temperament once more placidly engaged in whitewashing a house.

MEGGIE ALBANESI

ACCIDENT had decreed that nothing should take me to Fleet Street during that week-end in the December of 1923; consequently, I had heard no breath of rumour which might have prepared me for the shock of finding in the paper on the Monday morning an obituary notice of Meggie Albanesi—a notice which I myself might so easily have been called upon to write, had I happened to be on the spot when the news came in.

I stared at the page with a sense of stunned incredulity. I had known that she was ill—ill enough to cause the postponement of *A Magdalen's Husband,* the new play for which she had continued to rehearse, as we learnt later, long after she ought to have been on a sick bed fighting for life.

But Meggie Albanesi dead . . . repeat the words as I might, no real apprehension of their meaning would come to me. It seemed—it still seems—impossible to believe that the career in whose future triumphs all true lovers of the theatre had hoped to have their share was over already, cut off before it had even reached its prime.

There are some people in whom life seems to glow with so intense and concentrated a flame that we cannot imagine them dead, their flame quenched; and of these Meggie Albanesi was one. Among our youngest generation of actresses she stood alone. This one might be found attractive, that one promising, a third clever, a fourth beautiful; but when the real question rose, which, if any, of these young players might confidently be expected to develop into the great actresses of the future, the only name that seemed to have any insistent claim to be put forward was that of Meggie Albanesi.

"Intense"—that is the word which comes most naturally to my pen when I write of her. To every part that she played she brought the same power of imparting to a character, by the mere strength of conviction with which she played it, an inward glow of life. It seemed impossible to disbelieve in the least lifelike character when Meggie Albanesi played it, so vividly did she impress her own vitality upon it. Force of personality shone out of her eyes, and showed itself in every line of her small, dark, expressive face. I felt it when first I saw her, in a tiny part in *Mr. Todd's Experiment*. She had only one short scene to play—she did hardly more than flash into view and be gone, but there was in that fleeting glimpse something that set me groping and peering in the darkness to find her name in the programme.

Then came Mr. Galsworthy's *The Skin Game*, a play in which, as Jill Hillcrist, the daughter of the impoverished landowner, she got a real chance of showing the virtue that was in her. From that day she took her place, for me, in that small band of players whose names in the cast of a new play make the day of its production a theatrical event. Her next part strengthened my allegiance, proving her personal quality by sheer force of contrast. The play was *The Charm School,* an unpretentious American romantic comedy of the magazine story order, rather better written than most of its class. The part was that of a lovesick schoolgirl, and badly played might easily have become ridiculous; but Meggie Albanesi took the absurd creature and turned her into a human being who mattered intensely not less to us than to herself—and that was a piece of sheer acting magic. By a piece of poetic justice her reward came a few months later in the form of the chance to play Sydney Fairfield in *A Bill of Divorcement.*

Here was a part in which for the first time her powers were given full and free scope. Here was no question of being as good as her part would let her, but a real opportunity of showing how good she could be. The result was a triumphant success, which put her at one bound into the ranks of popular favourites, and made her name for the future one to conjure with. It is not likely that anybody who saw it will ever forget her acting in the scene where Sydney, having discovered that she has in her the taint of hereditary insanity, deliberately sets herself to "choke off" the young lover to whom she has only just become engaged. Once again it was by the still intensity of her manner that she achieved her effect. You could see little of her emotion, but you felt, as she went on deliberately and coldly inciting the unfortunate Kit to break with her, that she was tearing her heart to pieces. No other part in which I saw her—and the only one of her later parts that I missed was that of the Eurasian girl in *East of Suez*—gave her quite so fine a chance as this, but her playing in *Loyalties* and in her last part—of the plain but clever sister in *Lilies of the Field*—had the same quality of passionate conviction.

In the obituary notice to which I have already referred occurred the remark that Meggie Albanesi "had no great advantages in stage presence." The words struck oddly on my ear, but I realized that in the sense in which they were written they were true. She had neither striking beauty nor a commanding figure to capture the eye, no eccentricities of manner nor floridities of gesture to draw the attention. She was little, pale, and quiet. And yet the words, in the sense in which I should use them, were as untrue as they could well be; for when Meggie Albanesi was on the stage I had the greatest difficulty in keeping my eyes upon anybody else, and in her vital presence mere beauty suffered complete eclipse.

How high she was capable of rising in her art has now, alas! become a piece of empty speculation; but to me it has always seemed that she, alone of the young actresses of her generation, had in her that capacity for feeling without which no human being can become a supreme artist. Of her acting from the technical point of view I find myself now able to remember next to nothing. If you were to ask me if I thought her "clever," I should not know what to answer; "versatile," I suppose, she could not be called. But any such questions, in reference to her, seem unimportant and beside the mark; what matters is that she had in her a spark of that divine fire which, in the great artist, burns with a clear and steady flame.

That very spark, fed by the passionate love of beauty and of life which is the very essence of artistic genius, turned to a devouring fire and consumed her. She lived too intensely, and has paid penalty—to the deep and personal sorrow of thousands who, like me, had never known her except upon the stage. But this at least can be said, that in her short span of twenty-four years she had packed more of the joy of life than many of us are capable of feeling in a full three score and ten.

ON BEING CRITICIZED

EVERY writer, be his age nine, nineteen or ninety-nine, and be his subject what it may, has two fundamental reasons for putting pen to paper. The first is his firm and ineradicable conviction that he has something to say, coupled with a determination to say it to as many people as possible, and to keep on saying it as long as possible. The second is a desire to find out what other people think of it.

This latter emotion is a queer mixture of eagerness and shrinking. Authorship is much like child-bearing; and authors, like mothers, are touchy people. The proud young mother will present her new-born and amorphous offspring for your reluctant inspection, and want to know what you think of it; but if you told her honestly, she would never speak to you again. Just so the schoolboy shyly submits his first halting poem for parental judgment, but stands at his critic's elbow ready to snatch away his precious paper at the first word that is not praise. But the analogy does not go very deep. However frankly you told a young mother the horrible truth about her baby's appearance and general contours, however bravely she bore with your remarks, or forced herself to admit their justice, the discussion would not help her in the slightest degree to produce a better-looking infant at the next attempt. The young author, on the other hand, has usually the wisdom to realize that his offspring is not the result of obscure and uncontrollable processes of nature, but of a quite definite intellectual effort, the direction and control of which can be—or rather must be—learnt by force of experience. (It is true that I once knew a budding poet who was of the contrary opinion, and believed his poems to come into being by a species of parthenogenesis which he called "inspiration." Under the influence of this belief he not only proved exceedingly restive under criticism, but also refused point-blank to read the works of any poet other than himself, for fear of vitiating the purity of his conceptions. The result was natural, but not uninstructive; a bud of real promise became a wilted blossom, and failed to ripen into fruit at all.) Also, a baby is a concrete object; and the mother does not require the assistance of a critic to tell her whether her child is complete or not. A story is an abstract object. It exists in full completion only in the mind of its author, who tries by an arrangement of symbols on paper to convey it as completely as possible to his readers. Not until some of those readers have told him what impression his arrangement of symbols has produced upon their minds does the author know for certain whether, and how far, he has succeeded in expressing on paper the idea that exists in his own brain. The young author, therefore, depends on criticism to enable him to learn his job; and very soon he learns that undue sensitiveness to criticism must be mastered and brought under control. He finds that he must acquire polish by the friction of his own mind against that of the critic; and so by degrees he learns to be judged without resentment —perhaps even to be misjudged without rancour.

It is a curiously anomalous relationship, this between author and critic; for while it may be the author's duty to learn from what the critic says about his work how to do that work better, it is never the critic's business to set out to teach an author his job. The critic's scope is wider than that. Besides his duty to the author, he has his duty to himself and to his public; and these are all alike based upon his one fundamental duty of stating his opinion, and the reasons which lead him to hold that opinion. It is probable that in carrying out this duty the critic will find himself acting both as interpreter of the author to the public, and as revealer of the author to himself; but these functions are incidental and subsidiary to his main business of analysing and elaborating his own feelings towards the author's work.

But opinions differ. They vary in kind, in degree and in value directly as the tastes, the temperaments and the talents of the men by whom they are formed. The young author who has just published a book finds himself confronted with a huge, untidy heap of opinions of all sorts, shapes and sizes which he is called upon to sift—rejecting the chaff, but storing up the good grain to his own profit. While he is still unused to being criticized, he finds the task very nearly impossible. He reads through the pile, thrilling at the praise of one man, quivering under the censure of another. By and by he comes across a real "slating." He reads it, boiling with rage that his intentions should be so maliciously distorted, his ideas so deliberately misunderstood. If he were back once more in his father's study, he would snatch away his book and hide it. As it is. . . . The criticism may really be what he thinks it, a piece of callous cruelty on the part of a man who has seen a chance of being smart at the expense of a novice's blunders; but it may equally well be a scrupulously just estimate of the book's value, written by a first-rate critic with a habit of blunt speech. It is all one to the author. He goes about by day breathing out threatenings and slaughter against the offending critic, and spends the night in ecstatic dreams, roasting his enemy over a slow fire.

Then gradually he grows more hardened, and reaches the second stage. He develops (unless he is abnormally sensitive) a capacity for detachment; he learns to recognize and respect sincerity in his critics. He realizes, also, that it is to the adverse criticisms that he must look for real help. To be told how well you have done anything is, of course, very pleasant and very encouraging; but it does not help you to do it better next time. As I have said, the good that an author may hope to attain from criticism is polish; and the necessary friction between his mind and that of the critic can only be set up when the critic is not satisfied with the author's work. Under this process a writer finds that his rough corners are rubbed smooth. He realizes, for instance, that certain little mannerisms have an effect on his readers which he never expected or intended; and he drops them, to the instant improvement of his style. Then, as time goes on, he reaches the third stage. His detachment deepens into indifference; he has perfected his technique, he has gained such sure control of his weapon, and so nicely balanced an ability to judge its effects that criticism, in the ordinary sense, ceases to matter. Mr. Somerset Maugham, interviewed after *Our Betters* had evoked quite a storm of adverse criticism, simply remarked that there comes a time in an author's life when he writes solely for himself, and that after that point it makes no difference to him whether others like or dislike. This strikes me as an extreme way of putting things. If a miracle happened, so that everybody suddenly ceased to want to read Mr. Maugham's works or see his plays except himself, I doubt if he would remain quite unmoved in his secret soul; what he means, I take it, is really nothing more austere than the attitude to which Mr. John Galsworthy alludes in one of his short stories—"the neglect of the Press, which grows on writers from reading reviews of their own works." However, such Olympian serenity is impossible to the quick spirit of youth. The authors to whom criticism no longer matters hardly come within the scope of this article.

Supposing, then, that you are an earnest author who is determined to extract from the work of your critics anything that it may have to teach you; what hope have you of achieving thereby any real improvement in your art? Reluctantly I answer, very little, unless you are dowered with an equable temperament, or exceptional strength of mind. In an ideal world, every author would rise on stepping-stones of his dead self to higher things; but human nature is a sad destroyer of ideals. The whole business boils down to this. Any critic who impresses you as meaning fervently what he says is worth your best attention; if he further convinces you that what he says is right, then you are theoretically justified in reshaping your ideas, your style, or whatever it is, in accordance with his criticism. I am careful here to say "theoretically"; it depends in practice upon whether you can be trusted to make up your own mind or not. Some people are at the mercy of every specious advocate, and their opinion at any given moment is nothing but a reflection of that of the last person they happen to have been with. If you are one of these, heaven help you; once you begin listening to criticism you will try to follow in all directions at once, and will die a dizzy man's death. It is the cynic who will consent to take no man for granted that really benefits by criticism. If you are as wise, therefore, as you are earnest, you will not say to yourself that Mr. X. is known to be a fair and a far-sighted critic, and that accordingly, when you do not agree with his views on your own work, he is sure to be right and you wrong. Mr. X. is only human. In your particular case he may have been neither fair nor far-seeing. An irritating mannerism on your part, an injudiciously chosen lunch on his, may have jaundiced his view; or he may have a personal prejudice against the particular kind of book you happen to have written; or he may (once again, he is only human) have mistaken your meaning. You would be foolish, then, to think twice about a criticism which did not convince you, and more than foolish to let yourself be convinced without a struggle.

There remain for special investigation the whole-hearted diatribes of those critics who (it appears) would like nothing better than to see yourself and your book burnt together at the public expense. Your attitude towards these, whether they are unjust or merely ungentle, will again depend entirely upon your own temperament. There are some men upon whom a cold wind acts as a tonic, some whom it merely chills and depresses; and it is useless, if you belong to the second type, to expect to get any good out of cold winds. So with ruthless criticism—some people can stand it and others can not. Mr. H. L. Mencken, the American writer, is a cold-wind man. "A hearty slating," he says, "always does me good, particularly if it be well written. It begins by enlisting my professional respect; it ends by making me examine my ideas coldly in the privacy of my chamber. Not, of course, that I usually revise them, but I at least examine them. . . . But constructive criticism irritates me. I do not object to being denounced, but I can't abide being school-mastered." If your constitution is as robust as Mr. Mencken's, you can treat your "slatings" as he does: if not, you would be well advised to ignore them altogether. Not until you have scaled the calm heights of Olympus, and can breathe the same rarefied ether with Mr. Maugham and Mr. Galsworthy, will the cold wind of criticism cease to buffet you about; and if, on those lower slopes up which Mr. Mencken is climbing with chest bared to the breeze, whooping in sheer exhilaration, you find yourself shivering at the bite of the keen air, you must wrap yourself in your garment as closely as you may and climb doggedly on. "It is only mediocrities and old maids," said Oscar Wilde once in a review, "who consider it a grievance to be misunderstood." Like most epigrams, this is too sweeping a statement; like all good epigrams, it contains a solid core of truth. Sensitiveness under criticism is certainly no mark of the mediocrity, for many of our greatest men have suffered from it; but it is often the sign of a mediocre streak in the composition of a character otherwise great.

ONE MAN'S MEAT . . .

1. William Archer and Alexander Bakshy

I HAVE before me two books about the theatre, a big one and a little one, by two authors as violently opposed to one another in ideas and outlook as two men inhabiting the same world could possibly be. And while I am confident that the big book is a big book in more than the literal sense, and although I am by no means sure that the little book is anything more than just a little book, yet I am convinced that the late William Archer's *The Old Drama and the New* would have been a finer piece of work even than it is if it had not so utterly ignored the whole attitude and way of thinking that are revealed by Mr. Alexander Bakshy in *The Theatre Unbound*.

You will remember that in the Max Beerbohm caricature which represents the British Drama as a patient surrounded by disagreeing doctors, Mr. Archer's diagnosis was, " I don't think there's much wrong with her "; in this book he provides an elaboration and a defence of that diagnosis. He certainly does not think there is much wrong with her; in fact, he thinks that she has never before been half so healthy. To put it in his own words, " We are not living in a period of decadence, but of almost miraculous renascence." Mr. Bakshy, on the other hand, considers that the patient is practically lifeless.

"Will the nation that gave the world Shakespeare remain," he asks, "content with the utter degradation of its theatre, or, awakened to a new life, demand a new spirit on the stage—a greater spiritual and artistic significance in the drama and the form of its presentation?"

Without reading further in either book, you might safely assume that the demands which these two men make upon the playhouse are quite different. Both, it is true, want art; both want that "interpretation of life" which seems to be the one common factor upon which all theorists of the theatre are agreed. But the art of the stage to Mr. Archer means illusion, the creation of a mimic world, over whose fortunes and vicissitudes we fortunate mortals may brood with Olympian interest and Olympian detachment; while to Mr. Bakshy all illusion is anathema. "Poor playgoers of our day!" he exclaims. "Except in the music-halls, what consideration do they get in the modern theatre? They are only there on sufferance, having bribed the manager for the privilege of watching the show." To Mr. Bakshy nothing is pure theatrical art that dispenses with the direct appeal from actor to audience. The spectator must never be allowed to forget that he is at a play.

Listen to him:

"The theatre, if its object is real art, must, therefore, free itself of illusionism. It must shake off its slumber, forget its dreamy wanderings in the far-off realms of the playwrights' imagination, and come back to its own world —its Performance, its Showman, its Stage-boards, and its Spectators. . . . 'Performance,' now so unrecognizable in its ponderous representational garb, will appear in its divine nakedness. No longer will it be a picture of events as these are shaped in some real or imaginary world. It will itself be an event, but an event in the life of the theatre, a happening in that real world which is a gathering of actors and spectators come together, the first to practise and the second to watch the art of undisguised and glorying make-believe. Love and hatred . . . will be stage love and hatred. . . . The staginess of the play will mean an exhibition of life in terms of the theatre. . . . Nor will the playwright, in showing or presenting his drama, be bound by considerations of realistic, psychological, or some supernatural truth. His aim will be dramatic truth, and in bodying it forth on the stage he will be free to treat his material in any fashion he may choose so long as his convention is made intelligible, is theatrical in its nature, and lays no claim to be anything but a method of presentation."

Now hear Mr. Archer, in one short passage which really epitomizes the lesson of his whole big book:

"The true line of development lay (I suggest) away from Passion—that is to say, Passion for Passion's sake, Passion at all costs—towards ever more delicate and faithful Imitation."

The cleavage is, you see, complete; for the kind of performance to which Mr. Bakshy looks as the only thing to save the theatre would undoubtedly be stigmatized as a pernicious example of "Passion for Passion's sake" by Mr. Archer. In fact, the latter writer, applying his test of Imitation to our theatrical history, makes out the most complete indictment imaginable against the Elizabethan writers (Shakespeare, of course, excepted), proving them to be a barbarous and much over-rated lot; and the Elizabethans, if anybody in the world, used all the methods that Mr. Bakshy so ardently longs to see restored. Finally, in several places Mr. Archer goes further still, and reiterates his conviction that modern drama, so far from having fallen away from a high estate previously attained, "has cast out the foreign elements of rhetoric and lyricism, and become a pure art of interpretation through imitation"; and that "this purification is not a sign of degeneracy, but merely the last term of an inevitable and most desirable process of development."

It is the touch of—I hesitate to say complacency, and yet there seems to be no kinder word—revealed by this last remark that prevents Mr. Archer's book from reaching the very highest level of achievement. To say that drama has now reached "the last term" in a process of development is to imply that in one respect, at any rate, it can develop no further; it is perfect. But Mr. Bakshy's book points out many respects in which he considers that modern drama ought to be purified still further. Mr. Bakshy may be a bit of a crank; but he represents quite a large body of opinion, and there is much to be said for the views of him and his like, even by those who—like myself—would simply hate to have no theatre to go to but the one they would like to give us. I feel that in a volume of such scope, written with such brilliant scholarship and so wide a knowledge as *The Old Drama and the New,* Mr. Archer ought not to have allowed devotion to his own formula to lead him so completely to ignore a modern tendency to find that formula inadequate. He should have dealt with the modern anti-illusionists, if only for the purpose of putting them in their places as thoroughly as he has the Elizabethans.[1]

But when all is said, the important thing to remember is that Mr. Archer's theory and Mr. Bakshy's are not mutually exclusive, fundamentally as they may differ from one another. Drama is a wide field, in which many different methods of cultivation may exist side by side to produce widely different crops—which shall all, according to their several kinds, be good grain. Mr. Archer's crop may upset the digestion of Mr. Bakshy; Mr. Bakshy's would

[1] When these remarks first appeared in print, they drew from Mr. Archer a characteristic reply. He first dealt with my charge of complacency: "Mr. Darlington seems to hold that I do, in effect, prophesy when I say that, in the modern play of what may be called external realism, a long process of evolution has 'reached its last term.' But here he misunderstands me. I do not in the least intend to convey that the drama has touched its apex, or to prophesy for it a stagnant, unprogressive future. I should put on sackcloth and ashes before making any such forecast. In the realistic formula, greater men than those of the past or present may go on doing ever greater things; and other formulas may hold their own alongside of it. All I intended was a statement of strictly historical fact—that in the typical prose play (English and foreign) of the past thirty years a process of evolution had been consummated, and, on the mechanical or technical side, could no farther go. How far it may go on the spiritual side I do not pretend to guess; and I admit theoretically, though I scarcely believe, that it may have landed us in a blind alley, from which the future may have to 'try back.'"

He then went on to pick up the gauntlet I had thrown down, and to state his opinion of Expressionism. I quote his last paragraph, which puts his view in a nutshell: "That Expressionism will have some influence, possibly for good, upon the scenic art of the future, I do not doubt. But I do not think that sane criticism will get very much excited about it. Nothing, I am aware, is so exasperating to youth as the mild placidity of age; but I cannot pretend to be either enthusiastic or indignant when I feel no such emotion. Criticism, as distinct from ephemeral gossip, ought to fix its attention on the main current of development. Expressionism is an eddy."

certainly be pronounced unfit for human food by Mr. Archer. But as a matter of human experience there are people capable of thriving upon either—or both.

The real nature of the difference between the two can be quite easily analysed and defined. When Mr. Archer speaks of "the art of the theatre" he is thinking first of the playwright's work, and only secondarily of the work of the actor; and he himself calls attention to the fact that much modern criticism (including, as it happens, my own) has the same tendency. When Mr. Bakshy speaks of "the art of the theatre" he frankly means acting. For him the playwright merely exists on sufferance as the man who provides something for the actor to perform. There are other disciples of this school who hold that perfection in theatrical art will only be attained when the playwright is eliminated altogether, and the actor makes up his part as he goes along.

Mr. Archer accounts to his own satisfaction for the devotion of Lamb and Hazlitt, Leigh Hunt, and Lewes to acting by pointing out that they had no contemporary plays worth writing about. This may be true; but it does not explain away the fact that we still have critics who are equally interested in the acting and the play—Mr. C. E. Montague, for instance, and Mr. James Agate, and formerly (due allowance having been made for the fact that he is himself a playwright) Mr. St. John Ervine. There are no absolute rules of right and wrong in art; there is no dictating to any man what theatre he shall go to or why he shall like what he finds there.

2. James Agate and Harley Granville-Barker

It was a little odd that *Cymbeline,* which is by no means one of Shakespeare's best or best-known plays, should have been so very much in men's minds as it was during 1923. Few people attempt to deny that it is a ramshackle piece of work; some account for the poorer portion of it by saying that it was the work of a weary man, or of a collaboration. Yet we have seen a good deal of it recently. It was produced by the Old Vic as a matter of course. But, apart from that, it was done four times within a few months; romantically, in all sorts and conditions of costumes, by the New Shakespeare Company at Stratford; eccentrically, in modern dress, by the Repertory Theatre at Birmingham; fantastically, in clothes evolved by Mr. Bruce Winston from his own inner consciousness, helped by memories of the Russian Ballet, at the New Theatre; and (presumably—but I was not present) after the strict Elizabethan manner in the Maddermarket Theatre at Norwich. In addition, it was chosen as one of the first three volumes of the magnificent edition of the First Folio texts, still being published by Messrs. Benn Brothers, under the general title of *The Player's Shakespeare.*

A causerie-writer in one of the Sunday papers, writing about Miss Sybil Thorndike's production of *Cymbeline* at the New Theatre, called attention to the rough handling which this play had received from many of the dramatic critics. He printed a little list of the hard things that had been said about it in various papers, and they certainly seemed to add up to a general view that, in the opinion of the first-night house, Shakespeare ought to have been ashamed of himself.

For myself, I hold no brief for the play. I admit the unsatisfactory development of plot, the lack of drawing in most of the characters, the long-drawn-out tedium of many of the scenes. But I am always ready (and one or two of the gentlemen quoted by our causerie-writer are ready also—for extracts are misleading things) to bear with the rest of the play for the sake of Imogen. She is, to me, one of the loveliest of Shakespeare's women; and when, also last Sunday, I read the three cool sentences in which Mr. Agate dismissed her as "a poor pastiche," and assigned her "less wit than Rosalind, less gumption even than Desdemona, less resolution than Juliet," I felt myself in the presence of sacrilege. If the age of chivalry had still been with us, I should at once have mounted my charger and proceeded up Fleet Street to wind an insulting horn outside the offices of Mr. Agate's paper; and we should doubtless have adjourned to the gardens of the Temple and settled the matter with lances and battle-axes and those delightful clubs with spikes in the thick end.

As it was, I found myself impelled to sit down quickly and break at least a pen-nib in defence of my lady's honour; but at once I found myself face to face with a difficulty which, for the knights of old, simply did not exist. In mediæval times I should have found myself under no necessity to explain to Sir Agate exactly why I considered the Lady Imogen to be beautiful. I should simply have stated my opinion; and if I had subsequently turned out to be handier with the battle-axe than he, my opinion would automatically have become—so far as he was concerned—established fact. I had never analysed my feelings towards Imogen; I was simply conscious that she meant more to me on the stage than Desdemona or Juliet—perhaps even than Rosalind. Faced with the grisly duty of searching through the text to find out why I thought what I think, I picked up the new volume of *The Player's Shakespeare*. It opened at Mr. Harley Granville-Barker's introductory essay, and I began to read.

Having read, I realized that not even a pen-nib need be broken by me in defence of Imogen. Another was in the field—a more formidable champion, one better armed at all points than I; one who knew not only the extent of his devotion to his lady, but whence it came and wherefore she was to be accounted worthy of it.

"Imogen," says Mr. Granville-Barker, "is the life of the play. The best of the action either illustrates her fortunes or—directly or by contrast—enhances her character. . . . And it must be confessed we can feel him (Shakespeare), in her absence, labouring at his work somewhat conscientiously." This theme he proceeds to elaborate in nine pages of masterly analysis of her character. He says no word about her that he does not substantiate by reference to her own words or behaviour; he puts no reliance whatever upon his own unbacked opinion. Especially he points out how she gains lustre by contrast with each one of the other characters. One by one, he brings out of the text and sets in place her various attributes:

"She is clear-eyed and impulsive. Her very first words show it.

> Dissembling courtesy! How fine this tyrant
> Can tickle where she wounds! . . .

She has a touch of greatness in her, for she can go fearlessly to extremes. She is not, for a small instance of this, ashamed to show Pisanio how infinitely she loves her husband. She has a sense of humour about herself.

> I did not take my leave of him, but had
> Most pretty things to say.

She jokes to keep her courage up. She had obviously no real fear of 'the shes of Italy,' though later, in the overturning of the world of her faith, the joke comes back to her mind in earnest, as jokes will. She is a princess every inch of her; she has been used to giving orders from her cradle. But about herself she is humble-minded :

> My lord, I fear,
> Has forgot Britain.

She makes no more of it than this before the smiling Italian. But one can divine the 'For after all, who am I?' that would follow."

As Mr. Barker proceeds with his exposition we feel more and more strongly that Imogen is a character that would give life to any play. The above extract will serve to show that he writes interpretatively, from the producer's and the actor's point of view; and this perhaps accounts for the fact that where Mr. Agate finds negation—" less gumption even than Desdemona "—Mr. Barker discovers a shining quality : " She can be clear-eyed enough about the Queen, her father, or Cloten. But where she loves she trusts blindly, and even to the second degree." No wonder that where one sees only a poor pastiche, the other sees " a child of light." Every man to his own opinion; but to my mind's eye, Sir Agate lies unhorsed.

It is interesting to note how radically, even in their views on the versification of the play, these two men differ. Listen to them both, dealing with the same passage. Mr. Agate first:

"Even when Shakespeare obviously displays his hand he shows something less than his usual skill.

> 'Damn'd Pisanio
> Hath with his forged letters—damn'd Pisanio—
> From this most bravest vessel of the world
> Struck the main-top!'

reads like the poet who could make Othello talk of the butt and sea-mark of his utmost sail. But what are we to think of the succeeding:

> 'O Posthumus! Alas
> Where is thy head? Where's that? Ay me,
> Where's that?'"

Evidently, to Mr. Agate, this particular passage is nothing better than a piece of bungling, to be noted with sorrow and excused like Homer's nod. But Mr. Granville-Barker holds the contrary view, and states it with his characteristic confidence. He speaks of "the sheer physical horror which sends Imogen's quick brain whirling into hysteria," and by way of example he quotes (with the parenthetic eulogy "How amazingly well versified this is!") the whole of the passage held up to ridicule by Mr. Agate, with the addition of the next sentence:

> "Pisanio might have kill'd thee at the heart
> And left this head on."

Comment is needless—it simply remains to choose your side. This time, I must say, I find myself in the same lobby with Mr. Agate. Shakespeare may have been expressing hysteria, but it should not be difficult to find many other passages in which he does it to more moving effect than in this one. Miss Thorndike, at all events, got out of it no very memorable emotion.

3. Sydney Carroll and George Jean Nathan

Accident makes strange bedfellows. There is one shelf of my bookcase whereon stands a row of new plays and books on the theatre, waiting until I can find leisure enough from my other duties to deal with them. Side by side on this shelf, for no other reason than that they are both books of dramatic criticism, and chanced to reach me at the same time, stood for a month or so two violently dissimilar volumes—*Some Dramatic Opinions,* by Sydney W. Carroll and *The Critic and the Drama,* by George Jean Nathan. So completely do these two men differ in outlook and in method that I was at length impelled, by the very strength of the contrast, to deal with them in one article.

So far as I can see, they agree only upon one point—the fundamental doctrine that the critic must have a considerable amount of ego in his cosmos. Mr. Carroll's dramatic opinions are his own, and you are not required (or even encouraged) to agree with them. Indeed, a study of Mr. Carroll's writings while he was the critic of the *Sunday Times* has brought me the conviction, which a personal friendship with him has done nothing to allay, that he is never so happy as when he is in a minority of one, upholding with passionate sincerity some point of view which appears to his companions to be wrong-headed and extreme. Mr. Nathan has something of the same fighting spirit, but his weapon is more delicate.

I can picture either of these two men standing like a hero of romance at the head of a staircase and defending it against a crowd of assailants; but, while Mr. Carroll, clad in buckram, would wield an outsize club, and crack the sconces of his foes with whoops of enthusiasm, Mr. Nathan, in the silks and laces of one of those Bath exquisites with whom we renewed acquaintance at the revival of *Monsieur Beaucaire,* would flick at them with a rapier, wearing all the while an expression of ineffable contempt.

Mr. Nathan, indeed, is a kind of literary Monsieur Beaucaire—an aristocrat of letters, so conscious of his own superiority that he can find no better use for his skill than to irritate lesser men into making fools of themselves. He is an American; and he makes no attempt to conceal his opinion that very few American critics besides himself have any æsthetic perception whatever. But since, I take it, Mr. Nathan's victims are not very likely to admit to themselves the possibility that this Beaucaire who offends them may after all turn out to be of the blood royal, they are not likely to mend their ways because of his gasconading. The story of Monsieur Beaucaire would only be credible of a society in which snobbery had achieved an apotheosis—the hero himself being no less of a snob than his opponents.

Nowadays, as it seems to a detached, though

probably insular, Englishman like myself, the nearest analogy to the exclusiveness of the Bath of Beau Nash is to be found in intellectual America, where men (so I gather from reading American criticism and American novels) venerate incult knowledge as the men of Bath revered incult birth; where the pundits mistake real literary quality disguised beneath a pose of vanity, as Beau Nash mistook royalty disguised in plain clothes, for something lower even than it seems to be. In consequence, just as Nash's snobbery forced a prince who should have known better to play the snob himself, so the pundits of New York and Boston have driven Mr. Nathan to make something of an exhibition of himself. He allows himself to be pushed into saying things that are absurd, not because he thinks they are true, but because he is determined to flout and annoy his opponents.

Here is an extract from his book:

"It is commonly believed that the first virtue of a critic is honesty. As a matter of fact, in four cases out of five honesty is the last virtue of a critic. As criticism is practised in America, honesty presents itself as the leading fault. There is altogether too much honesty. The greater the blockhead the more honest he is. And as a consequence, the criticism of these blockheads, founded upon their honest convictions, is worthless. There is some hope for an imbecile if he is dishonest, but none if he is resolute in sticking to his idiocies. If the average American critic were to cease writing what he believes and dishonestly set down what he doesn't believe, the bulk of the native criticism would gain some common-sense and take on much of the sound value that it presently lacks. Honesty is a toy for first-rate men; when lesser men seek to play with it and lick off the paint they come down with colic."

I am afraid that Mr. Nathan is here guilty of taking his own advice, and dishonestly setting down what he does not believe, for the purpose of confusing still further those writers whom he terms imbeciles. Translated into bolder, but plainer, English, the passage just quoted only means that four out of five American dramatic critics have not an opinion of their own worth listening to, and, therefore, would be well advised to copy those of wiser men (Mr. Nathan himself, for example). That may quite possibly be a true statement of the condition of things in America —I am in no position to have an opinion—but it certainly does not justify Mr. Nathan in drawing the conclusion that the critic's first quality is not honesty. Indeed, Mr. Nathan gives his little game away in an earlier chapter of this same book, where he says: "The concern of art is with beauty; the concern of criticism is with truth."

If all criticism is statement of personal opinion, as Mr. Nathan and Mr. Carroll agree in postulating, then the fundamental requirement is that it should be honest opinion. Honesty by itself, it is true, gets you nowhere—observe the effect of the honest blockhead's opinion upon the temperamental Mr. Nathan! A critic must have, besides honesty, the ability to form serious opinion for himself (that is, taste), and the ability to express it when formed (that is, style). When a critic is fortunate enough to possess all three qualities he is the first-rate man of whom Mr. Nathan speaks. When he possesses the second and third in a supreme degree (for there are no degrees arguable in the matter of honesty) he is numbered among the great. But, though he speaks with the tongues of men and of angels and hath not honesty, he is become as sounding brass or a tinkling cymbal.

Mr. James Agate, who is Mr. Carroll's successor on the *Sunday Times,* once pointed out in a preface that the important thing in criticism was, not what you thought, but how you expressed it: "Our knowledge of Kean and Kemble comes to us through Hazlitt, who, for all we can swear to the contrary, may have been mistaken as to these actors' graces and parts." There is one thing, however, that we *can* swear about Hazlitt—that, mistaken or not, he meant and believed most honestly every word that he wrote about Kean and Kemble and the rest. You can swear the same about Mr. Carroll, agree with him or admire his methods or not as you may; you cannot take the oath with the same certainty concerning Mr. Nathan. Obviously, he can be dishonest on occasion. If you wish to give him the benefit of the doubt, you can say that he shares Mr. Carroll's propensity for rushing into battle on the side of the minority, but personally, I do not believe it. I suspect Mr. Nathan of a tendency to be too clever, which, if persisted in, will prevent him from taking any very high position among those first-rate men of his. Once again let me adapt the words of St. Paul, and conclude with a text for writers of criticism: "And now abideth taste, style, honesty, these three; but the greatest of these is honesty."

PERSONALITY AND TEMPERAMENT

"ENJOYMENT of personality is one of the principal allurements in the theatre." This sentence was written recently by a dramatic critic in the course of some laudatory remarks about a certain popular actress—a lady whose abundant personality, as it happens, neither exercises allurement upon me nor causes me enjoyment. I quote the dictum here as a sort of text, chiefly because it is devastatingly true; but also because its truth is calculated to affect different people in widely different ways. About the use and abuse of personality in our theatre centres the great and never-ending conflict between the interests of Art and those of Popularity. Actors (like other artists) are born, not made. This does not mean, as so many aspiring young novices seem to think, that if you have acting in you you can walk straight on to a stage and proceed to witch the world as Hamlet; but it does mean that if you have not a potential Hamlet somewhere in you when you first attempt to act you will never be able to manufacture one, however hard you try. Certain gifts every aspiring actor must have from Heaven; and of these the two chief are personality and temperament.

A man's "personality" is his power of being himself; and, in the narrower stage sense of the word, an actor of personality is one who has developed the power of making himself appear to advantage under the glare of the footlights. This power is naturally seen at its highest pitch on the music-hall and revue stage, where—to all practical intents and purposes—personality is the only thing that counts. When you go to see Mr. George Robey, for instance, you go frankly to see Robey. You do not worry particularly about the plot of the entertainment he happens to be in, still less about the character he plays. You have heard from a friend, or read in a paper, that Robey has some good material in "Hocus-Pocus" (or whatever it is) and you go off happily to buy the tickets. And if, having bought those tickets, you were to discover that the great George had discarded his eyebrows and all that they stand for, and was acting (say) Macbeth in all seriousness—well, you would feel yourself aggrieved. Even if Robey's Macbeth proved to be a sound and earnest study, you would, I take it, still feel aggrieved. That is the penalty of personality which all great music-hall entertainers have to pay. Grock, for instance, may nourish in his secret heart an ambition to play leading parts à la Sacha Guitry. If he does, he must keep it secret—or else begin again from something very like the beginning. The Grock of the Coliseum stage we all know and love. The Grock of private life is a different being altogether, known only to a favoured few.

If, some day, the Coliseum public arrived on a Monday afternoon to see their bald-headed, spindle-legged idol; and if, instead, the Grock of private life appeared and began to play—as well as ever you like—the man's part in *Un Monsieur Attend Une*

Madame, I should expect the ensuing scene to be more gratifying to the evening papers than to Sir Oswald Stoll. Now the austere critic's chief complaint against the stage of to-day is that too much of this spirit has crept into the legitimate theatre. He laments that this, that, and the other popular actor can in truth play only one part—himself; in other words, he laments that this, that, and the other actor is not an actor at all, because he lacks temperament.

"Temperament" is a queer thing to define, especially since the word is so often misused. To many minds "a temperament" means simply a useful scapegoat invented by vaguely artistic people in order that they may turn their lapses from the rules of common-sense and self-control "to favour and to prettiness." With that kind of temperament, as exhibited by the April Mawnes and the Mary Westlakes of this world,[1] I am not here concerned. Temperament—since I must attempt some kind of definition if I am to get any further—is that essential quality in an actor which enables him to merge his own individuality in the character of another man, and so appear to be other than he actually is. In a sense this quality is the exact antithesis of personality; for personality is the power of being most particularly oneself, while temperament is the power of becoming somebody else. The antithesis is not complete, however. No actor, however lavishly he may have been dowered with temperament, can really become another person; he has to make use

[1] See p. 107 *et seq.*

of his own personality to supply the deficiency. The two qualities, therefore, instead of being mutually exclusive, must exist side by side in the artist; and the measure of that artist's personality will be pretty nearly the measure of his popularity with the big public, while the measure of his temperament will be that of his reputation with the critical few.

This explains the fact that here and there you will find men (women, too, of course) who are what is called "critics' actors." These are people whose temperament is all that can be desired; but their own personality is lacking, or deliberately suppressed, or, if present, is not found quite sympathetic enough by the ordinary playgoer. Their work is praised by the discerning, but is to some extent "caviare to the general." The name of one such man occurs to me now as a case in point. Personally, I should not hesitate to bracket his name with those of the accepted leaders of his profession; yet he seldom or never plays a leading part. He is generally to be found playing an important, but secondary, part in London somewhere; and I have yet to see him make a personal failure. In each new part he undertakes he seems to become a different man—not merely in appearance, but in the atmosphere he creates; and I believe that it is owing to this very fact that he has so far missed the popular fame that he has deserved many times over. He sinks his own personality in his part; and people remember his parts but forget his identity.

This was proved to me a short time ago in a striking way. In conversation I happened to mention this particular man as being one of the best living English actors, only to find that my companion (a man keenly interested in the theatre, but with too many calls upon his time to be able to go regularly to the play) could not remember to have heard of him. And so a first-rate artist remains —except to the few—in the second rank of his profession, and sees exuberant third-raters promoted over his head; men and women who combine with the merest trickle of temperament an overwhelming tide of personality.

It is a half-understanding of this state of things, I suppose, which leads many hasty but intelligent people to deny to players of the Hawtrey or du Maurier type all credit for "acting." They admit the power of personality in these actors but call their temperament in question. It is true that the whole technique of a Hawtrey or a du Maurier is based upon the possession of a strong and attractive personality; but it is not less true that behind that technique there is at work a strongly interpretative temperament, quick to understand and convey by means of that technique the finest shades of thought and emotion. All characters played by Gerald du Maurier are expressed for us by means of a whole battery of small personal tricks and habits of speech and gesture which can be labelled and pigeon-holed separately in your memory; but for all that you cannot say of any one such character, "This man is du Maurier himself and nothing else." His Dearth in *Dear Brutus*, his Hubert Ware in *The Ware Case*, may look the same, speak with the same attractive accent, move with the same lazy grace; but they have not the same feelings, nor do they affect you in the same way. In each play the actor has been explaining to you not himself, but somebody else in terms of himself.

This "somebody else" is generally understood to be the character as originally conceived by the author, but in reality it is never exactly that—even in the hands of an abnormally sensitive and conscientious "critic's actor." It is the author's character as re-conceived by the player; and the manner of its re-conception varies with the player's personality. In effect, the "critic's actor" says to the author, "I will show you how your character would behave in the flesh"; while the actor of strong personality says, "I will show you how *I* should behave if I were a man like that." The dramatist who is essentially a literary man, and only by accident of choice or opportunity a writer for the stage, would probably prefer to be interpreted by the "critic's actor";[1] but the dramatist who writes for

[1] See Mr. A. A. Milne's confession in the introduction to his *Three Plays*: "So much for Mr. Shakespeare. I differ from him (as you were about to say) in that I prefer to see my plays printed, and he obviously preferred to see his acted. People sometimes say to me: 'How beautifully Mary Brown played that part, and wasn't John Smith's creation wonderful, and how tremendously grateful you must be.' She did; it was; I am. . . . But the fact remains that, to the author, the part must always seem better than the player. . . . So when John Smith 'creates' the character of Yorick, he creates him in his own image—John Smith-Yorick; a great character, it may be, to those who see him thus for the first time, but lacking something to us who have lived with the other for months. For the other was plain Yorick—and only himself could play him. Alas, poor Yorick, I knew him well, a fellow of most excellent fancy. Would that you could know him too! Well, you may find him in the printed page . . . or you may not . . . but here only, if anywhere, he is to be found."

Mr. Milne is here writing himself down as a maker of books who has somehow strayed into the theatre; and incidentally he is,

the stage because he has a special gift that way, who realizes that his play is only half finished when he has laid down his pen, would choose the other. He knows that the character ultimately seen on the stage must be, not simply his creation, but the joint creation of himself and the player. He knows that his best work, in the hands of a player possessing temperament and nothing more, can prove great only if he (the dramatist) has made it so; and he knows that in the hands of a player of great personality —say of an Eleanora Duse—his work may be transmuted into something rich and strange, and be made to glow with a splendour beyond his most ambitious dreams. For it is temperament that makes a man an actor, but personality that makes an actor great.

very gently and with as little show of violence as may be, biting the hand that feeds him—the hand of John Smith. Yorick is a character in a play. When Mr. Milne drops his pen Yorick is alive just so much as, and no more than, Galatea was alive when Pygmalion laid aside his chisel. The gods did for Pygmalion much what John Smith does for Mr. Milne; and I seem to remember that Pygmalion complained in similar terms that in bringing Galatea to life the gods endowed her with all kinds of attributes not possessed by his statue. An ungrateful crew, these artists!

INEVITABILITY

THERE are two kinds of inevitability with which the playwright has to deal. One is a quality—it may be the greatest quality in a great play; the other is a defect so serious that it is almost bound to cripple any play in which it crops up. In each case the inevitable thing is some incident in the play which the audience can foresee, though the characters cannot. But here the likeness ends. The higher kind of inevitability is a mark of fine craftsmanship, the lower of bad or careless craftsmanship. Possibly it may be as well to begin by defining this latter more clearly, and so pave the way for consideration of the former.

An excellent example of the wrong kind of inevitability occurred in *I Serve*. This was a play which was well conceived and cleverly written, and yet failed altogether to be impressive. It dealt, you may remember, with an ex-maidservant (wonderfully played by Miss Edith Evans) who devotes her life to an attempt to bring up her illegitimate son as a gentleman, like his father. Obsessed with this idea, she nearly wrecks the lives of herself and the three other chief characters of the play. As the action of this play proceeded at its first performance, I became more and more certain in my own mind that the author was leaving himself only one possible method of ending his tale—the easy, obvious, and utterly unconvincing method of killing off the son. A glance at the programme confirmed this suspicion; I found that the son was not among the characters of the play.

Now it is quite a legitimate and effective way of acquiring merit on the stage for a dramatist to pretend that he is going to be inevitable and obvious in this sense when really he has an unexpected trick up his sleeve all the while. Mr. Milne's final scenes in *The Dover Road* form an excellent example of this. He brings your heart into your mouth for a moment or two by making you think he is going to finish his play with a commonplace and very stagy tucking up of loose ends, by making Anne fall into the elderly and unsuitable arms of Mr. Latimer. Then, at the last minute, he extricates himself with such deftness that an end which would have been very effective anyhow is rendered doubly effective.

A more recent and even more striking example of this occurs in the last act of Mr. Lonsdale's *Spring Cleaning*. At the beginning of that act the wife has every intention of bolting with the (secretly reluctant) *tertium quid;* and it is quite obvious that the *tertium quid* will fail her, and she will go back to her husband in time to bring the curtain down upon a happy ending. I imagine that when the curtain went up upon the last act on the first night of this play, there was not a single member of the audience who did not know exactly what was going to happen.

For myself, I am free to confess, I settled down to watch a commonplace and probably rather perfunctory act, whose course I felt I could foreshadow with a fair degree of accuracy; and, in common with the majority of the audience, I had the most complete surprise imaginable. The author did exactly what he had led us to expect of him, but he did it in a way that nobody expected. The *tertium quid*, instead of letting the lady down and being kicked out of the house by the husband in the good old obvious way, proceeded to extricate himself with delicate impudence from his awkward position, and to dominate the act to the extent of stage-managing the reconciliation between husband and wife. This act, with its achievement of the right kind of inevitability and its extraordinarily deft avoidance of the wrong kind, made the success of the play.

There was no such deftness in *I Serve*. I watched it draw nearer and nearer to its conclusion, hoping all the time that the dramatist would find some less obvious solution to his problem than the death of the son. With a sinking heart I heard that the boy had gone to Australia; and when, later on, I was told that he had embarked on his homeward voyage I lost hope both for him and for the play. Both duly sank.

The dramatist's mistake did not here lie necessarily in the mere killing off of the character. From the first it was inevitable (in the better sense) that before the curtain fell the author must get rid of him—so far, at least, as his mother's obsession of making a gentleman of him was concerned. The problem before the dramatist really was how to get rid of the son to the best effect, whether that entailed killing him off or making him marry a barmaid in Australia and settle down as keeper of a saloon (if that is what they call public-houses in Australia). The mistake lay in the fact that the playwright shirked his problem, and allowed the son's death to occur owing to a pure accident, quite extraneous to the plot; that is, he relied on coincidence when there was no need to do so, and managed that coincidence so clumsily that the man in the stalls could see it coming afar off. What he should have done, I take it, was to arrange that in some way the disappearance of the son arose naturally out of the plot; he might have contrived, for instance, that the mother's harping on the idea of his growing up a gentleman had driven the son to marry a barmaid out of pure perversity.

Curiously enough, Mr. St. John Ervine's play, *The Ship*, gives an example of the right dramatic use of this very incident of the drowning of one of the characters in a wrecked liner. The whole action of this play centres upon the struggle between a famous shipbuilder and his son, who wishes to be a farmer instead of carrying on the family tradition. When, therefore, the father—by means not quite honourable—forces his son to represent the family on the trial trip of a new unsinkable liner, which nevertheless sinks, he seems to be reaping the consequences of his own overbearing egotism. There is a touch here of the true tragic inevitability—that attribute of which I began by saying that it may be the greatest quality in a great play; but hardly more than a touch; for, after all, it is a strange coincidence that on the first and only voyage that young Jack Thurlow makes the ship should strike an iceberg, while John Thurlow, his father, in his sixty-two years of life among ships, must have made many such voyages without encountering a disaster of the kind.

This higher inevitability is the very essence of the old dramatic rule of thumb, that a playwright must not keep secrets from his audience. "We feel strongly," says Professor Bradley, "as a tragedy advances to its close, that the calamities and catastrophe follow inevitably from the deeds of men, and that the main source of these deeds is character"; and he goes on to state that while the dictum that with Shakespeare "character is destiny" is no doubt an exaggeration, it is the exaggeration of a vital truth. It will be seen at once that inevitability in this sense is something very far from obviousness, though it has, if I may put it so, a kind of retrospective obviousness. In a play of any serious pretensions, whether its ending be happy or not, the climax is as often as not foreshadowed from the very beginning. The playgoer's preoccupation is not with the nature of the climax so much as with the means of reaching it. If the playwright is to succeed he must reach his climax by a succession of stages which should certainly not be obvious to the spectator before they are reached, but should yet seem the logical and inevitable outcome of the actions and reactions of the characters with regard to one another.

It is easy to guess when Shakespeare first shows you Beatrice and Benedick crossing rapiers that he is about to extract delicious comedy from the story of how Signior Montanto and his dear Lady Disdain are gradually transformed into a pair of true lovers. How it is to be done you do not know, and during the process you are kept continually wondering what is to come next; but at the end you find that the destined climax has been reached by a route so cunningly and convincingly devised that it seems to be the only one possible. If this is true of comedy it is much more true of tragedy. It is in proportion as the playwright manages to convey a sense that some brooding fate is waiting, hidden but inevitable, for his central figure that he succeeds in making his tragedy ring true.

In the little world of his invention the dramatist is a god. He can bring his creatures to good or evil as he wills. But in doing so he must show the aloof ease and the calm omnipotence of a god, or he will lose his godhead. Like other gods he must let the men he makes seem to come to grief through their own follies, their own disobedience to the unchanging laws, their own excesses of character. If he himself is seen to be taking a hand in the game, sinking ships and so forth to gain his private ends, his power is seen to be a finite and contemptible thing, and his worshippers vanish.

THE STAGE ACTRESS

A GOOD title should, I suppose, be self-explanatory. It should combine the qualities of a bill of fare and a cocktail; it should tell you what you are going to have to eat, and at the same time whet your appetite. To these requirements, I am only too sadly aware, the title of this essay conforms very imperfectly. It is ambiguous; there are several things it might equally well mean. Hence I am reduced to the clumsy expedient of employing an opening paragraph to tell you what it actually does mean—to explain that my subject is not the "stage" actress as opposed to the "screen" actress, nor, indeed, any kind of flesh-and-blood actress at all; but the actress considered as a stage character.

Authors seem to enjoy setting actors to act actors. Plays have been written in plenty round the personalities of historical players—David Garrick, Nell Gwynn, Peg Woffington, Deburau, and so forth. It might be interesting to make a complete collection of such plays, and compare them in detail—but that would call for the expenditure of a good deal more knowledge, time, and patience than I have at command. I only want to compare two recent plays which have actresses as their chief figures. These two plays are *Advertising April* (by Messrs. Herbert Farjeon and Horace Horsnell), in which Miss Sybil

Thorndike appeared at the Criterion, and Mr. St. John Ervine's light comedy, *Mary, Mary, Quite Contrary*. In some ways, these two plays are so alike as to make it a most remarkable coincidence that they should both have reached the public at practically the same moment. The likeness is accounted for, I think, by the fact that all the three authors are, or have been, dramatic critics.

The man who takes up the profession of dramatic critic begins, after a time, to look upon actresses with an eye in which delight and admiration is blended with a certain disillusionment. He is too much of a man of the theatre to regard them with the distant and excited worship of his youth; on the other hand, he is not sufficiently a man of the theatre to share in the freemasonry which links together all those whose work lies behind the footlights. In consequence, he occupies an anomalous position between the world of the playgoer and that of the player, sharing the pet illusions of neither. He hears the intimate gossip of the theatre, how this famous actress behaves like a spoilt child at rehearsals, how that famous actress never knows her lines, how a third famous actress cannot make a single gesture on the stage unless it has been laboriously explained to her beforehand; but he hardly ever penetrates behind the scenes, or meets the ladies of whom he hears so much. Gradually he inclines to the cynical generalization (which I have heard stated again and again) that brains are a hindrance rather than a help to any actress who wants to be a popular idol.

You may see this belief at work in both the plays under review. April Mawne in the one play, like

Mary Westlake in the other, is an utterly preposterous person according to any normal standard, and lives an utterly preposterous life. You are given a common factor in the two plays, of a heroine who lives by the caprice of her own "temperament," instead of by the light of ordinary good sense; and it is curious to notice how like causes beget like results. Each lady has to be attended by a rather blatant man of business, whose purpose in life is to see that due attention and respect is paid to the star's so valuable "temperament," and to exploit her personality to the public. April has her husband and press agent, Eddie Hobart, whose dual identity makes most of the trouble in the play; Mary has Mr. 'Obbs, her manager, described as "a good-natured, unimpressionable vulgarian—the only man in her experience who has not been imposed upon by Mrs. Westlake." Each lady has an infatuated youthful admirer with poetical leanings; and each admirer (this paragraph is beginning to be reminiscent of the ancient trope beginning, "As I was going to St. Ives") is loved by a modern young woman of his own type and social station, only waiting till the actress has finished with him before reclaiming her property.

There, except for a few accidental details, the similarity ends; the themes of the two plays are entirely different. You can see this from the two titles, which have all the qualities which I have confessed that mine, above, lacks. Messrs. Farjeon and Horsnell deal with Hobart's methods of advertising April; their play is a satire on publicity-mongers. The actual character of April herself, however well drawn, is a secondary consideration. Also, she is not really "temperamental" at all. Hobart says she is, because the public expects it of an artist; she herself probably thinks she is, because any girl who has been thoroughly spoilt by success, and is in a position to get her own way whenever she cares to try, is bound to give at times an exhibition of capriciousness in the sacred name of artistic temperament. Actually she is a good-hearted girl, slightly stupid, but quite shrewd, who—but for her film-face—would have settled down to contented and heavy domesticity in the suburbs.

Mr. Ervine, on the other hand, is concerned chiefly to draw the character of his contrary Mary—a true portrait of a temperamental woman. His methods are necessarily more subtle than those of April's creators. Mary's young poet, for instance, is a real young man, who might have written a fine dramatic poem about Joan of Arc; April's Mervyn Jones, who rhapsodizes about bathing in forest pools at twilight, is an amusing stage caricature. These two men give you the ratio of the two plays; or, as a mathematician would put it tersely, Geoffrey Considine : Mervyn Jones = *Mary, Mary: Advertising April*.

Mary is put before us as a woman of real eminence in her profession. Beeby, the popular playwright, who boasts that he has made a large fortune by completely ignoring the human mind, says of her: "She is a very unusual woman. I do not know any human being whom I detest so much as I detest her." To which somebody replies: "But you want her to act in your play?" "Yes," says Beeby. "She has few rivals as an actress." I think, therefore, that I am justified in taking Beeby's evidently disinterested opinion as embodying the author's own view of Mary Westlake's acting. As to her person, she is described in the stage directions as "a beautiful actress, with an artificial manner which is entirely natural to her." She appears at Hinton St. Henry Vicarage (Geoffrey's home), and proceeds to set everybody by the ears. She monopolizes Geoffrey, much to the grief of his cousin Sheila, who loves him, and makes no secret of the fact. Mary gets him to promise to take her out in a boat after dinner (which Sheila angrily describes as "moonlight paddling," a phrase which is curiously reminiscent of Mervyn Jones and his twilight pools). Then she changes her mind, and takes instead Geoffrey's uncle, Sir Henry Considine, a retired Colonial Governor; she proceeds to lose the oars; she and Sir Henry drift out to sea and are picked up by a trawler, arriving back at the Vicarage in the morning covered with mackerel scales. In order to preserve Mrs. Westlake's reputation, both Geoffrey and his uncle propose to her. She accepts them both—subsequently explaining that she nearly always accepts proposals of marriage because "people look so pathetic when they're proposing to you, and I haven't the heart to refuse them." Then Sheila appeals to her, and Mary turns down both Geoffrey and his play and departs, making a "good exit" by promising Sheila a contract as soon as she is safely engaged to Geoffrey—"and when he signs the register in church the day you're married, you can ask him to sign the contract too."

I had been hoping for a long time that Mr. Ervine

would write us a comedy, when *Mary, Mary* . . . appeared; and having read it, I was unreasonable and ungrateful enough to be disappointed. The play is amusing to read; it acts well; its central character, as Miss Eva Moore has shown us, is one which gives a first-rate comedy actress chance after chance; but still my disappointment persists. I had expected Mr. Ervine's comedy to be more subtle than this—not in characterization but in plot. His happenings seem to me too hectic for his people and his general atmosphere. Mary behaves as preposterously as April Mawne, without being able to claim the excuse of having been conceived with a touch of burlesque.

In fact, I believe in Mary Westlake, but not in the things she does. As I have hinted above, I know very few actresses, and none with any degree of intimacy;[1] but I try to imagine the eminent Miss Dash and the admired Miss Blank going down to a country vicarage to read a play. I can see either of them behaving, in general, just as Mrs. Westlake behaves; talking too much, spreading charm everywhere in the way of the men, and getting themselves hated by the women. But—I may be quite wrong—

[1] It will perhaps come as a surprise to many people to realize how little the dramatic critic (as distinct from the theatrical journalist, whose business lies largely behind the scenes) has to do with his victims. It certainly came as a surprise to me. In my youthful days I had an idea that the dramatic critic spent his life in a giddy round of temptation, being courted and flattered by stars and bribed by managers. Now, after more than five years spent in the exercise of this pampered profession, I have with sorrow to record that nobody has ever attempted to cajole or corrupt me. Had any done so, I trust that I should have been proof against their blandishments; but it is really rather dull never to have been put to the test.

I cannot see them getting engaged all round on arrival, and losing oars by insisting on rowing in choppy seas, and generally making hay as Mary does. If Mr. Ervine wanted to get a little innocent fun out of improbable incidents, he shouldn't have made his people so real; for they are all human beings with a real claim on our sympathy (at least, I'm not quite sure about Miss Mimms, the Girl Guide; and I have never yet seen a young woman with her heart stitched quite so firmly to her sleeve as Sheila's is, though I'm ready to believe I shall some day). Mervyn Jones would have been much more at home in Mr. Ervine's plot than Geoffrey Considine is.

STAGE FORM

FORM in drama appears to be determined mainly by two factors—both external and accidental, in the sense that the artist has little or no control over them. The first factor is the theatre in which the play is to be represented; the second is the audience before which it is to be performed. The peculiar characteristics of Greek tragedy, for instance—its formality, its austerity, its declamatory character, its lack of action, its poetic perfection—are the natural outcome of the circumstances in which it was produced; of the fact that it was intended to be acted in an open-air theatre, devoid of mechanical accessories, before a huge audience of a very high standard of culture. Similarly you can explain the special qualities and defects of Elizabethan drama in the light of your knowledge that it was intended for a theatre situated in or carefully modelled on the inn-yard of the period, and for an audience whose power of æsthetic appreciation was as quick as it was crude. And so on.

In every age the actor, the theatre, and the audience have come into existence before the playwright, who has therefore been compelled to conform to an established state of affairs, and to shape his play accordingly. In every age the critic, coming after the playwright and studying his methods, has been faced with the temptation to formulate those methods into a code of arbitrary laws, and to judge not merely his own theatre but those of every other time and place according to his own code. Aristotle must be declared exempt from this temptation, because he was concerned in the *Poetics* only with his own theatre, from the best of whose practice he deduced certain principles; but the innumerable disciples of Aristotle who, time and again in the history of the theatre, have brandished the Three Unities in the faces of the unfortunate playwrights of their own generation, and have demanded "so and no otherwise shall your plays be written," have proved themselves thereby to be critics of little vision.

Even so great a critic as Dryden, living in a cocksure and undiscerning age, allowed himself to temper admiration for Elizabethan drama with a feeling that Shakespeare would have been a better playwright if he, too, had sat at the feet of Aristotle. But, just as surely as the form of Shakespeare's *Antony and Cleopatra,* with its multitude of short scenes, was determined by the inn-yard pattern of his theatre, its platform stage running out into the auditorium, and its almost complete lack of scenic devices, so surely was the shape of Dryden's *All for Love*—a fine copy, but a copy nevertheless, of Shakespeare's play—determined by the fact that the English playhouse had now developed under French influence into the earliest form of the modern "picture-stage" theatre. With the introduction of painted scenes, it became the playwright's duty, in the interests of his play, to avoid shifting his ground more often than was absolutely necessary. As scenery grew more easy to handle, the structure of plays became less rigid, until with the scientific and mechanical discoveries of the nineteenth century the Unities, though paid a considerable amount of lip-service by theorists, were once more disregarded by practising dramatists.

You have only to look at the history of Shakespearean production to see how profoundly the shape of the theatre influences that of the play. Every generation of men of the theatre since Shakespeare's time has acknowledged his greatness by staging his plays; but no generation except his own—and perhaps our own—has made any attempt to produce his plays as he wrote them. The Restoration theatre paraphrased his plays; the theatre of Garrick "improved" them (both with the very laudable object of making them conform to the shape of the kind of play then being written); and the Victorian theatre, still with the same laudable object, "arranged" them for production on a large and magnificent scale, with all the latest innovations of lighting and scenery.

We, to-day, have gone back, as nearly as is compatible with adequate decoration, to the uninterrupted continuity of action which the Elizabethans enjoyed—and are inclined to be unduly puffed up about it. You may hear people to-day talking in superior tones of the vandalism, the self-satisfied philistinism, of the men who dared to set their judgment above Shakespeare's. It is easy for us to talk; we have not the difficulties to overcome that they had. Taste changes from generation to generation; and we have something in common with the Elizabethans that neither the eighteenth nor the nineteenth century had. In Mr. Walkley's phrase, we are an " untidy " generation, to which rigid form is anathema; and since " the plays of Shakespeare (it was the real gist of Voltaire's complaint) were untidy," [1] we naturally like to see them produced in all their untidiness, and pour scorn on those who would tidy them up. But perhaps we do well to take all the credit we can get; for the next tidy generation that comes along will put us firmly in our places. What will it have to say, for instance, about our inability to act the plays of the eighteenth century in the grand manner?

However, I must leave Time to bring in its revenges, and return to the contemplation of the difference between our fathers' methods and our own with regard to Shakespeare. Since we have more innovations of lighting and scenery even than they had, our producers ought logically to be trying to outdo in grandeur the scenic effects in which Irving, or Tree, or Forbes-Robertson won their laurels. Instead, spectacle has gone just a little out of fashion. It moves no longer in the highest dramatic circles. Its place nowadays (except here and there, in a play such as *Hassan,* which lends itself specially well to large-scale productions) is with the slightly less exalted ranks—melodramas, revues, pantomimes, and the like; in fact, with those forms of dramatic entertainment in which the telling of a story is not the prime consideration.

New factors have come into operation, chief among which, I believe, is to be reckoned a new

[1] *Still More Prejudice,* p. 205.

desire on the part of modern audiences for speed. Playgoers of the past generations, pleased with the mechanical devices which were then a novelty, were content to sit patient through long and frequent intervals while the scenes were changed. To-day playgoers will not sit patient through any intervals at all, except the one or two breaks which the frailty of human nature demands in a long performance. Mr. Robert Atkins and Mr. Bridges-Adams can make their big scenes as elaborate as they please, but only on condition that the play is kept going in between.

From this demand for continuous action springs another feature of present-day stage decoration—the permanent setting, without or with scenery. The Phœnix setting is an example of the former, that for *The Duenna* of the latter. The whole aim is to eliminate intervals, and the result is bound to be that dramatists will feel themselves free to write plays of a much less rigid form than consideration for the taste of the public, and still more for the pockets of their managers, has allowed them to attempt hitherto.[1]

I have no doubt in my own mind that the chief influence upon dramatic form at the present moment is the competition of the films. Plays are costly things to produce, and depend for success upon an immediate appeal to their public. It follows, then,

[1] Indeed, such plays are already being acted, and are proving a thorn in the flesh of producers who do not happen to have modern scenery at command. When an expressionist piece, *The Dance of Life*, was staged at that solidly Victorian playhouse The King's, at Hammersmith, there was one scene which was considerably shorter than the intervals which preceded and followed it; which was very depressing.

that the public theatre (which, however high its artistic ideals, must depend in almost every case upon the box-office for means to live—men like Sir Barry Jackson being scarce) must be influenced by alterations in the public taste. That taste has been profoundly modified of late years by the film. A picture-house is cheap, it is comfortable, and its entertainment is continuous. A theatre which has to meet such competition must have something very definitely better to offer than its rival, and it must, where it can, meet its rival upon his own ground.

There are certain advantages which the stage has over the film which no degree of mechanical perfection can ever hope to neutralize—the living personality of the player, the presence of his emotion and the expression thereof by his voice are the chief of these advantages. In the matter of continuity the stage is showing itself well enough able to hold its own. But when it comes to the question of spectacle, the stage is hopelessly beaten from the start. The film-producer can, and does, pile spectacle upon spectacle without interfering with the action of his story. Elaborate scene succeeds elaborate scene in a manner to turn the stage-producer green with impotent envy. The stage-producer must choose between speed and spectacle, and has chosen speed. How right he is I discovered the other day, when I went to see a stage play written by a film-producer of some note. True to his training he had set his action in nine scenes, most of them fairly elaborate, and as the curtain went down and again down, leaving me to my solitary meditations, I cursed the day when scenery (or the cinematograph) had been invented.

STAGE ENGLISH

SOME little time back, being in a self-indulgent mood, I bought myself an exceedingly neat and most business-like wooden tray (as used by all Napoleons of finance on the films), whose purpose in life was to sit on my desk and hold such papers as I judged to be of particular interest. In this way, I hoped, I should be able to keep my very unmethodical mind up to the scratch. All my outstanding correspondence, all the letters and comments from readers and friends which might give me material for articles, all the miscellaneous collection of notes, memoranda and newspaper cuttings that had heretofore lain about my desk in an untidy mound which was the despair of my domestic staff—all this would now go into the tray and be instantly at hand when required.

Well, it was a delightful notion; but unfortunately it does not work out in practice. You cannot make an unmethodical person like me into the complete business man simply by presenting him with a business man's gadgets—you only make his last state worse than his first. In the days of my untidy mounds, I did at least know approximately where to find a paper when I wanted it. Nowadays, any paper I want is buried fathoms deep in the tray, which is the one place in the house where I never can remember to look for it. All of which is designed to explain, if not to excuse, the fact that I am now sitting down to write an article concerning a letter which was posted to me months ago, was put on one side as raising a point of general interest, and was discovered by me in the tray, quite accidentally, at the beginning of the present week.

However, except for the fact that my correspondent must by now have lost some of the first fine flush of indignation which impelled him to write (indeed, since he wrote from a big London hotel, it is probable that he has long since returned to his native America), the letter has lost nothing by keeping. It deals with a problem that we who love the English theatre have always before us, and deals with it trenchantly, as you shall hear. " My dear sir," the letter begins, " I went to a play the other night after reading your criticism of it, in a theatre where the stalls cost twelve shillings, and found the principal actors enunciating their words in a manner which was slovenly to the point of being sometimes partly unintelligible, as well as offensive, to the æsthetic ear. Yet you had said no word in reprobation, nor do I recall cases in which your colleagues on other London journals have done so in similar instances."

Here I pause to protest that to some extent my correspondent wrongs both my colleagues and me. Over and over again I have read, or written, criticism in the London Press concerning the slovenly habits of speech into which our actors have fallen, adjurations to English players to speak up and speak distinctly, sorrowful comparisons of the looseness of our standards in this matter with the precision of the French. But, all the same, it is a melancholy fact that in the particular instance in question it had not occurred to me to remark on this " slovenly, unintelligible, offensive " pronunciation, and obviously, therefore, it could not have struck me as being any worse than usual. In other words, the standard of speaking on our stage at present is so low that it takes a more than usually dreadful exhibition to rouse the case-hardened critic to more than an occasional protest in general terms.

Of course, if I liked, I could reply to my American correspondent by suggesting that he has a very fair-sized mote in his own eye; because I have heard some astoundingly bad speaking from American players who are not without honour either in their own country or in ours. But I have no intention of taking any such line, because the plain fact is that both Americans and English, however they may compare one with the other, come off very badly when you consider their elocutionary standards beside those of the French. The fundamental reason is the same in both cases. Put as plainly as possible, it amounts to this: the French, as a nation, speak their language well, the Americans and ourselves do not.

You have only to compare the contemporary novels of the three nations to realize the truth of this. When an English or American novelist wishes to draw a thumb-nail sketch of a casual individual belonging to any but the best-educated classes he gets his effect by spelling his character's slovenlinesses of speech phonetically—by making it clear that the man in question tortures his vowel-sounds, swallows his consonants, drops his aspirates, and so on. The French author cannot get the same effect in the same way. Only when he is drawing peasant types, or foreigners, or other abnormally queer speakers does he mutilate his spelling; because he knows that the average middle-class Frenchman speaks—not, perhaps, the best French, but good French. The consequence of this is that the half-educated French boy who goes on to the stage has a far better chance of learning to speak his language perfectly than an English or American boy of the same type.

But even education, in England at any rate, does not solve the difficulty. There is, I suppose, a definitely accepted standard of speech in this country, to which everybody is expected in theory to conform; but, as a matter of fact, so few people conform to it that they are liable to be looked upon as pedantic. My American correspondent remarks on this, quoting the Poet Laureate as his authority. "He said, as I recall, that in England, and certainly in London, there is often a tendency, even among some of the people of the so-called higher circles, to pronounce all the vowels more or less alike, crushing them into a sort of diphthong. . . . The consonants, more especially those which are final, are often not pronounced at all, or at least without much help from the tongue, lips, and teeth, and we frequently find nicely-dressed folk who seem to assume an air of superiority because they pronounce an 'r' as though it were a vowel. This bad practice is naturally reflected on the stage."

Here my correspondent certainly flicks me on the raw; for I am quite conscious that I am as consistently guilty of swallowing my "r's" as the next man—and, when you come to think of it, there is really no logical reason why to drop an "r" should be any less awful a crime than to drop an "h." At all events, I am convinced that we shall not get back to a decent standard of speaking on the stage until actors break away from the present convention of imitating the little careless tricks which disfigure the casual conversation of those of us who have never learnt elocution. That is to say, we need to get right away from the present idea that it is an actor's business to speak on the stage the English of ordinary life; because the one great fundamental duty of every actor is to be heard. So long as he is indistinct, or fails to speak loud enough to be heard by his audience, he is no good for the stage—though he may yet be destined for greatness on the film.

In our fathers' time the convention went too far in the opposite direction. Actors' diction grew too "stagy," too full of exaggeration, and became an accepted subject for the humour of the comic papers. It is from the overdone precision and pomposity of those old actors that we are now suffering a strong reaction. The younger generation of players have identified themselves so closely with the young man of the period that they now talk even more like him than he does himself. This sounds, I am afraid, like an over-statement, but it is a fact that some of the best, clearest, and most careful stage diction that I have heard on young men's lips lately has come, not from professionals, but from amateur players at Oxford and Cambridge.

WHAT THE PUBLIC WANTS

WHAT *does* the public want when it goes to the theatre? If there were any really satisfactory answer to that question, London would become so full of theatrical managers that there would not be enough public to go round. There are a good many theatrical managers about as it is; but a large proportion of them are soured and disgruntled individuals who, having attempted to gauge the popular taste with varying success, snort at the very mention of the public, and complain that it simply doesn't know *what* it wants. In this they do the public less than justice. It knows what it wants well enough; like the crocodile in *Peter Pan,* it "knows and yet it can't say." Confronted with a particular play, it very soon delivers its judgment; but it is an inarticulate monster, lacking the power of speech to make its likes and dislikes known except by forcing those who would tickle its appetite to adopt a clumsy and costly system of trial and error.

It is commonly supposed that the dramatic critic's business is to act as mouthpiece, and so make the monster articulate; but this is a fallacy. The dramatic critic can only act as spokesman for himself and that section of the public which happens to share his views; and the very fact that he is a dramatic critic with special knowledge and wide experience of every kind of drama makes it unlikely that his views will coincide with those of the comparatively uninstructed. The critic, in fact, goes to the theatre in quest of something for which the average playgoer cares less than nothing; not from the critic, therefore —except it be from Mr. Flawner Bannel—will the answer to the question come. Indeed, it seems that the mystery will remain for ever unsolved; and brave men will continue to risk fortunes upon their ability to guess the answer, and many will lose everything, as in the past. Still, on the off-chance that it may have a value to somebody, I will contribute my mite of experience in this matter.

This spring a certain suburb in South London, which is go-ahead enough to hold an annual literary festival (after the model of the eisteddfod in Wales), honoured me with an invitation to act as judge in its one-act play competition. I accepted the invitation with some misgiving, and in due course I presented myself at the local town hall, prepared to do my best. The plays performed were six in number, and I will describe them to you succinctly in tabular form:

(*a*) A fantasy, wherein a young girl is faced with a choice between two future selves—the one described as "A Stately Dame" (rather a snob, between ourselves); the other a gipsy with repulsive habits, but a feeling for nature. There is a kind of literary convention that in such circumstances the call of nature shall always outweigh the claims of civilization, and so I was not surprised when the girl forsook her home and an inconsiderable lover to be off with the raggle-taggle gipsy, O.

(*b*) A short farce, brightly written by a gentleman who seemed to have taken for his motto: " When writing for the stage, be stagy above all things." Where but on the stage could be found a collection of bachelors, presumed sane, who would pledge themselves never to marry except on the drawing of lots, and then to wed within the year? It is a mark of the low esteem in which so many people hold the theatre that an educated audience will sit complacently through performances of far-fetched stuff such as this without turning a hair.

(*c*) A rather sentimental little play concerning two brothers, one crippled, the other in full possession of his strength; but the cripple was good, while the other was a very bad hat indeed. The plot hinged on the theft by the bad brother of his father's cash-box, and its discovery by the cripple; but the chief quality in the play was a marked promise in character drawing which the author displayed.

(*d*) Another fantasy—better thought out and written than (*a*), but so poorly acted that its possibilities were lost. When I came to remark on this play at the end of the evening I made a mildly jocular remark to the effect that if Sybil Thorndike had been acting in it I should probably have thought it the best play of the series—and the local Press subsequently reported me as having said it was a part well suited to Miss Thorndike!

(*e*) A playlet on the " Time Machine " idea, in which two young lovers are transported back to the Garden of Eden. Amusing in parts, but with no dramatic movement about it.

(*f*) A penny dreadful. A terrific tabloid melodrama, with a guilty wife, a coldly implacable husband, a lover, a pistol, a death. Handled with an eye to stage effect only, logic being completely abrogated; the events of the play not even proceeding out of one another. It was acted—quite rightly—after the finest Elephant and Castle tradition.

Adjudication, as you may imagine, was no easy process. None of the six plays was good enough to be judged by any very searching standard of criticism, and they were so different in kind that I could find only one way of comparing them at all—namely, to ask myself which I would best like to see again. Looked at from this point of view, (*b*) and (*f*) were at once ruled out. What virtues they had were superficial and of the magazine-story order. (*a*) was too slight to bear searching examination, (*e*) too lacking in clarity. The only real promise of good work for the future that I could discover was in (*c*) and (*d*); and of the two (*c*) had far more of what is, in my view, the dramatist's paramount virtue—sense of character. I therefore awarded the prize to this play.

There is a sequel to this—a sequel not without its instructive side. Before I made my comments on the plays and announced my award, the audience were asked to vote which of the six plays each member liked best; and in due course the result of the plebiscite was forwarded to me. It ran thus: (*f*) 132 votes; (*e*) 65; (*b*) 38; (*c*) 36; (*a*) and (*d*) nil. After every possible allowance has been made for personal prejudice and errors of judgment on my part, it is obvious that this order of merit does not, and never could, agree with mine. It is true that I had made a conscious effort to discount the acting, and to judge only the play, and that I had therefore previously read the plays in manuscript; but I doubt if even this made very much difference. When that list was sent to me I saw at once that the great majority of an educated audience had responded to some quality in the plays which had left me comparatively cold. I soon saw what this quality was. The popular vote had arranged the plays in exact order, according to their air of possessing incident, of causing bustle, of making things happen. Ideas counted for nothing, form for nothing, character for nothing; crudeness of thought, of composition, of psychology were no drawback. The Elephant and Castle School had won, hands down.

Well—since *vox populi* is *vox dei* nowhere more certainly than in the theatre, there is a strong probability that the Elephant and Castle partisans are right. All plays are compounded of three elements—plot, style and character. The popular play has any amount of plot to a halfpennyworth of character and no style; the kind of play usually condemned as "literary" has any amount of style, some character, and no plot; the ideal play has all three. The student of drama, the man who sees as many plays in the year as an average playgoer can visit in a lifetime, very soon exhausts the pleasure to be found in plot—for there are said to be only seven different plots in all the world—and finds himself relying more and more upon the infinite variations of character. He takes the plot so much for granted that he fails to worry his head particularly if it is not there. None of the plays that I had to adjudicate was an ideal play; only (*c*) had any pretensions to draw character, only (*d*) had any glimmering of style; these accordingly had my vote. But (*f*) and (*e*) and (*b*) had plot—or, at least, incident. These, therefore, came nearest to being what the public wants. It is idle to point out that there is no right and wrong in these matters; I am not concerned to justify myself in the eyes of those with whom I do not happen to agree. They have as much right as I to have their tastes catered for in the playhouse. This article is no more than a hint to the playwright who wishes to draw the public, that when he takes up his pen he should not look to the Needy Knifegrinder as his dramatic model. He must make sure, before he begins, that he has a story to tell; having done so much for the sake of the public, he may safely proceed to add the other ingredients to suit his own taste.

AMATEUR ACTING

IT is over a century since the owner of Mansfield Park returned from Antigua to find his house given over to preparations for " theatricals," and—much to the relief of scandalized Fanny Price and the hardly more complaisant Edmund—proceeded to crush the godless scheme. Jane Austen herself (who might, if she had lived now, have been a great dramatist instead of a great novelist) was as shocked as her heroine at the frivolity, almost amounting to depravity of mind, that could suggest such an idea to the inhabitants of a decorous English mansion. Since that time actors and acting have both gained steadily in prestige, until nowadays " the " profession ranks almost as high as " the professions," and the young woman of the period dabbles in some form or other of dramatic expression as inevitably as Jane Austen's young women dabbled in painting or music. The term " Amateur Acting " covers an enormous field, from the casual charade to the full-dress performance in a West End theatre, and from unsophisicated " private theatricals," where the musty conventions of the Victorian stage maintain their last precarious hold on life, to performances of all but professional perfection such as the Old Stagers give at Canterbury. The love of dressing-up and make-believe seems to have been implanted in almost every human being, and there must be few men indeed with souls so dead that they have never pretended to be somebody else. But not until recently has there been any real recognition of the value of this universal dramatic instinct. Between the professional and the amateur stage there has always been a great gulf fixed; there is a bridge across it, it is true, but of so light and flimsy a structure that for every ambitious amateur that has fared safely across, many more have fallen into the abyss. In all ages and in all arts the professional has been apt to sneer at the "gifted amateur"; yet, by all but the favoured few, the first steps must be taken in amateur work of some kind. The number of stage "stars" who found their true bent while acting as amateurs is very great; so much anybody can prove by reading any stage reference book. Many famous actors have had their first experience of their art in the dramatic clubs at their universities; and these are men of a type and temper that the stage could ill afford to lose. There seems every reason to suppose that the supply of such men in the future will be even greater than in the past. The strong modern tendency towards the practical recognition of the value of drama in education ensures that; certainly the dramatic work which is now being done at the two great universities has a reality and a force which are new to it, and which nobody can afford to ignore.

One of the vexed questions in the theatre-world of to-day concerns the right of entry into the profession. At a time when many theatres are closed and many tours abandoned, and when unemployment is rife in consequence, the number of young and inexperienced aspirants trying by hook or by crook to get a footing on the stage is still as great as ever. Various remedies are proposed, but not one is free from serious drawbacks. Some men pin their faith to the reorganization of the stage on trade union lines. That is to say, they wish to regulate supply in accordance with demand, and prevent unemployment by reducing the numbers of the employable. According to this idea, nobody could go on the stage without first obtaining some kind of diploma authorizing him to do so. Nobody would be allowed to act who had not graduated from one of certain accredited dramatic schools. The "gifted amateur" with money and influence to back a small or non-existent talent (that bugbear of the out-of-work professional) would be got rid of completely by such a scheme. But many people object to the products of the schools, saying—and saying with reason—that no course of academic study can make an actor; only acting experience before audiences can do that. The fact of the matter seems to be that acting, like every other art, lives by uneconomic methods. You cannot deal with an art as though it were a trade. The actor's profession can be organized like a trade, or it can be recognized as an art and left to go its wasteful way. But in proportion as it is treated as a trade it must suffer as an art, and so far as it is allowed to be an art it must be unsatisfactory as a trade. The amateur actor, who may or may not develop into a professional, is nothing but a noxious weed in the trade unionist's neat garden; but he may be a very healthy plant from the point of view of art. Art has no boundaries; it is common ground, in which every human being has the right to labour according to his skill and his leisure. Nobody can forbid the amateur author or painter to pursue his particular form of expression, and if his writings or paintings are good enough to be bought in the open market before those of the professional, that professional has no right to complain. He is himself at fault for not writing or painting better. In the world of art the aristocratic principle reigns supreme. Those who are at the top matter a great deal; those at the bottom must prove their fitness by survival. The achievement is the only thing that matters; whether the man behind it is natural genius or trained craftsman, rich or poor, working for his living or for the pleasure of the work, matters nothing. The trade unionist necessarily views the profession from the bottom of the ladder, which has the natural effect of causing the crowds who struggle round the lowest rungs to bulk largest in his sight. On behalf of these he is concerned to eliminate unemployment, to secure a living wage, to keep out the encroaching amateur; and he can leave the great ones to look after themselves. But these things are nothing to the artist compared with the danger that a stage so organized might lose a potential Ellen Terry.

PLAYS AND BOOKS

THE BROTHERS CAPEK

I HAD almost headed this essay *The Czech Drama*, since the brothers Capek are acknowledged to stand together at the head of their profession in the new Czecho-Slovakian Republic, and since their works are the only specimens of Czech dramatic writing that London has yet seen. But my immediate purpose is to consider those two remarkable plays *R.U.R.* and *The Life of the Insects* side by side, and try to discover their common factors; and such factors are more likely to prove common to the Capek family than to the Czecho-Slovakian nation.

" Remarkable " is, I think, *le mot juste* in connection with the Capeks' work. It defines with some exactitude their quality and their limitations. Their work is indeed " remarkable," and little more. Both the plays that I have mentioned are intriguing, arresting, out of the ordinary; when they were running in London, nobody who was interested in the theatre could afford to miss them. But that either of them represents real progress in the art of writing for the theatre I am prepared to deny categorically. Each of them is completely lacking in the quality which I believe to be the first (perhaps the only) essential of great drama—knowledge of and love for humanity. The Insect Play sets out to satirize human nature, and fails to do so as successfully as it should because it only manages to establish a comparison between the insects and such exaggerated types of mankind that we ordinary sinners are made to feel that all this is no concern of ours. The satire is entirely negative in its effect; the good qualities of the human race are not examined, but quietly ignored.

Some time back I was invited to the Hippodrome to witness some wonderful juggling with the spectrum by M. Samoilov. This gentleman introduced his audience to a normal young woman with red hair and a summer frock, and a normal young man in a lounge suit. Then he snapped off the normal lights and turned on his newly-invented set which was designed to shut out certain rays, and, behold, before our eyes, the young woman was transformed into a black-haired Oriental dancer, and the young man into a gorgeous and no less Eastern rajah. We applauded and were pleasantly thrilled at M. Samoilov's cleverness, though I for my part could not see that his invention was likely to prove of any very great practical value; for, change colours as he might, he could not change form. After the first shock of surprise was over it was clear that the summer frock and the lounge suit were still present under the Oriental patterns which the new lights had picked out upon them.

The Brothers Capek seem to have found for themselves a similar new light in which to survey humanity; the ray which in their case is shut out is the one which illuminates the soul; and, since it is only in the possession of souls that human beings are usually understood to be differentiated from the lower orders of creation it naturally follows that the Brothers Capek can see no essential difference between ourselves and those lower orders. They see us as creatures of shallow passion and shallow poetry, like the butterflies; of unreasoning, sordid, and profitless greed, like the beetles; of cruel, mechanical efficiency, like the ants; of high and beautiful hopes that come to nothing, like the may-flies.

And, again, after the first shock is over, it becomes plain that this is just another piece of jugglery with another spectrum; that beneath the insect-like traits picked out by the satirists the form of the human soul can still be descried, destroying the illusion for the man who still retains the clear use of his eyes.

But when once this protest on behalf of the finer side of human nature has been made, it must be confessed that the satire gets home thrust after shrewd thrust against humanity's baser elements. The butterfly has served many a poet as an image of beautiful care-free happiness; but a human being with the desires of a butterfly will be an airy trifler, whose life consists in transient emotions and centres round a cocktail bar. The beetle—that peculiarly depressing species which spends its life collecting malodorous balls of dirt, wherewith presumably to stock his larder—has stood to us before now for an example of honest thrift; but a human being with the desires of a beetle will have no interest in life except to make his "pile," and to begin collecting another as soon as the first is complete. The ant gave Solomon the text for his rebuke to the sluggard; but the human being who has the desires of an ant will be concerned only with ceaseless, useless work which is destined to end in aggression and destruction. Here is a mordant indictment of society idlers, of profiteers, of Kaiser and Soviet; but the withers of mankind as a whole are unwrung.

More general in its application is the indictment hinted at in Mr. Playfair's sub-title to this play, "And So ad Infinitum." That happy little pair Mr. and Mrs. Cricket are ruthlessly killed by the Ichneumon Fly to feed his daughter, the voracious Larva—who in her turn is killed and eaten by the Parasite; and even Mr. Cricket is not outside "the simple law, the common plan," for he has only secured the little home to which he is bringing his wife by the fortunate accident that another of his kind has selected just the right moment to be eaten by a bird. In the midst of life, say the Brothers Capek, we are in death. The Chrysalis which rhapsodizes, through three acts, of the great things which it will do when it is born turns into a May-fly, dances a moment in the sun, and dies; and the Tramp, who acts throughout the play as a human interpreter to point the moral to the audience, dies in the end—owing, we are left to suppose, to intensive entomology in the cold night on an empty stomach; but also, we cannot help suspecting, because the Brothers Capek were a little at a loss how else to bring their parable to a close. Personally, I did not find that the parable probed deeply enough into my conscience to send me home from the Regent Theatre vowing to live a less lepidopterous life for the future.[1]

[1] But even so, I found *The Insect Play* far better worth seeing than half the plays that have made successes in the last few years. As a piece of stage work, apart from its novelty, it gives its producer great scope and its actors little. On the whole, Mr. Playfair and his helpers rose to their opportunities. The butterfly act, which is much the slightest so far as the writing is concerned,

In *R.U.R.*, the play which Karel Capek wrote without his brother's collaboration, I found the same lack of human understanding cropping up in a different way. Here it manifests itself in the simple fact that not one of the human characters in the play really lives. Harry Domain, Helena Glory, Dr. Gall, Alquist, and the rest are all (with the possible exception of the minor character Emma) as much the puppets of Karel Capek's brain as the Robots are said to be of Dr. Gall's. I was far more interested in the Robots than in the humans when I saw this play, and I did not care a blow when the latter were all killed off at the end of the third act, so long as we had the Robots to carry on with.

I feel that a writer of real stature would have made of this annihilation of the human race an almost unbearable tragedy. If Helena Glory had been a real woman, instead of a shadowy figure bodying forth Karel Capek's idea, the manner of her death would have been a stark horror. There is a certain relevance to this point also in my feelings about the last act, in which two of the Robots develop

lacked the appeal to the eye that it might have been given; but the Creepers and Crawlers scene was splendid. Most of the acting chances come in this section of the play; for the Ant act is purely a piece of collectiye effort, calling only for strength of lung in its chief characters. It is amazingly effective, however. The blind time-keeper who sits in the middle of the stage, and never ceases counting the beats as the unending stream of ants passes, each busily intent on doing absolutely nothing; the furious shouting and restless pacing of the leaders; the bustle and hurry of the declaration of war, and then the armies of the ants filing by in another endless stream to death, still in step to the beating—all this, against the dreadful industrialized background of chimneys and telegraph wires, weighs down the mind and afflicts the nerves with an all but intolerable sense of the helplessness of the individual in the grip of a highly organized community spirit.

sex-consciousness and the sense of beauty, and bring the play to an end with a promise of the birth of a new race that could almost be called human. First I had this scene described to me by an enthusiastic member of Mr. Dean's staff, and thought it sounded wonderful. Then I read the play, and thought the scene considerably less wonderful. Then I saw it staged, and did not like it at all. In theory, it is wonderful; in practice, it lacks humanity—without which no play can be more than technically effective.

It is here that *R.U.R.* falls short of such a play as Ernst Toller's *The Machine-Wreckers*. Both plays treat of the relations between man and machinery; but while Toller preaches strongly the doctrine that only man matters, Capek is obviously more interested in his machines. No. "Interested" is too weak a word. He is obsessed by his machines. He regards them with fascinated horror, with the same fear as the people in *Erewhon,* which might very well be the liberary source of this play. This horror of machinery and mechanical civilization appears also in the diabolically effective Ant act of the Insect Play. It comes to this. Capek has a real enough concern for humanity and the future of the race; but to have a concern for human beings is by no means the same thing as being able to create them for the stage.

In an article on the Czech Drama, based upon facts supplied by Mr. Paul Selver—who translated both the Capek plays into English—Mr. W. R. Titterton stated an ingenious theory to account for the "universal" character of these plays. "Like the Czecho-Slovakian Republic," he says, "the art of the Czech has attained its independence, and can now afford to be international. Only when nationality is unquestioned can it be safely ignored. The revulsion from local associations was likely to be extreme; and so we find it, for the men and women of *R.U.R.* are not citizens of any particular State; they are mankind."

This is clever and sounds logical; but I cannot help feeling that it is based on a slight confusion of thought. That strongly national literature comes from countries whose national consciousness is made sensitive by a position of dependence, is quite true—Wales and Ireland supply examples near at hand, and the Czech theatre in the days of German domination supplies another very much to the present point. But I cannot believe that the young Czech Republic, prosperous as it is, can have become already so accustomed to its independence as to ignore nationality.

And, as a fact, these Capek plays do not ignore nationality. There is a fierce consciousness of nationality running through them both, taking the form of a revulsion from nationality. Where these two plays touch the question at all, they are not non-national, but anti-national. The Ant act is anti-national, and so is the passage in *R.U.R.* where Domain puts forward his idea of making national Robots for the future, and is told that it is "horrible." Now, violent anti-nationalism, like violent nationalism, argues not an ignoring of nationality, but an abnormally sensitive consciousness of nationality; just as the deplorable old roué with a taste for unclad chorus girls and the excessively pure-minded maiden lady who drapes the legs of her chairs are displaying each an equally abnormal consciousness of nudity. I have little hope, therefore, in Mr. Titterton's implied conclusion that the Capek brothers are to be the pioneers of a new drama of world-wide importance. Mr. Paul Selver himself seems to have as little. Speaking of Karel Capek, he says: "Of the influences which have helped to shape his ideas, perhaps the war has left profounder effects than literature, for from it his logical mind has derived a whole series of destructive tests to apply to society and civilization." If there is one thing necessary to a man's success as a pioneer, it is surely that he should not be a pessimist.

To sum up, I feel that these Czech plays have not much real significance, apart from their intrinsic interest as being a little off the main stream of writings intended for the stage. They represent a backwater, interesting to explore and exciting enough in itself, but leading nowhere. It is only in the main stream that real progress can be made; only by creation of human beings that the great plays are written.

THE EXEMPLARY THEATRE

THE Exemplary Theatre, after which Mr. Granville-Barker's new book has been christened, is an edifice which does its enthusiastic architect very great credit. It is very beautiful, and very complete. Not only does it shine in the sun with a delicate and unearthly beauty, but it is finished to the last bath-tap. It has everything that you (or, rather, Mr. Barker, for tastes are bound to differ in this as in other things) could desire—except foundations to connect it with this solid and workaday world. It is Mr. Barker's vision of the theatre as it might be, his dramatic Cloudcuckooborough. "Castle-building it had better be," he says at the beginning of his second chapter. "One could plan for the development of work already in being. . . . But it will be more to our purpose to imagine in broad outline a theatre as school, fulfilling its widest mission under the most exacting circumstances, and to beg the question of how it could be brought into being. Details will give verisimilitude, and they are half the fun of castle-building." He won't be happy, you see, without his bath-taps.

"A theatre as school"—that is the important phrase. He wants to see his theatre occupying, besides its status as a playhouse, the position of an educational institution such as the London

School of Economics or the L.C.C. School of Architecture. In this school intending actors, playwrights, or critics would be able to study every branch of the theatrical art on the theoretic side; while the fact that the building containing the school could "accommodate two fully-equipped and actively working playhouses" would ensure that the practical side is not to be neglected. Mr. Barker develops his ideal theatre on each side, as school and as playhouse, with a minuteness which you must read the book to appreciate; but when all is done, I find myself more impressed and interested by the implicit criticism of the theatre as it is than by the explicit description of the theatre as it might be.

Mr. Barker's chief interest in the stage is an interest in acting; though he is careful to render due lip-service to the art of the playwright. About acting, therefore—what it is, how it is learnt, and still more what it ought to be and how it might be learnt—he has a great deal to say that everybody who is interested in the theatre should read. It is Mr. Barker's chief complaint that under present conditions the actor receives no stimulus towards the finer shades of his art; if he is boldly effective and obvious he is received with shouts of applause; if he is concerned to "cultivate the niceties of restraint and delicate workmanship," nobody but himself and a few colleagues are any the wiser for his achievement. Critics and public alike, he considers, know nothing of acting and care less; they must be taught both to know and to care.

I do not think that Mr. Barker can be said to have here avoided the special pleader's commonest faults;

he overstates his case, and he tends to assume that his doxy is, as a matter of course, orthodoxy. He speaks of critics with a sad, gentle resignation—regarding them as men who have little chance of doing good work under modern conditions, but fail to take even that little. As to the public, well, his attitude is defined completely by a single sentence of his own: "Few things can debauch an art so much as the lack of any decent standard of public taste."

But a man with a mission may perhaps be allowed to overstate his case, so long as his case is a good one in itself. Mr. Barker's certainly is. He gets at the root of the matter when he points out that quality in acting depends on a faculty for appreciation in the public. "Granted a good audience," he says, "good acting of a sort must result." I am much less impressed with Mr. Barker's schemes for the education of his actors than with his ideas for the evolving of playwrights, critics, producers, and a knowledgeable public. The first thing that is needful is a "good audience"; public taste may not perhaps be quite so bad as Mr. Barker thinks, but at any rate it ought to be better. The only thing that can make it better is the recognition of the drama as an essential part of education.

This, indeed, is the chief value of Mr. Barker's book, that he keeps hammering away in an attempt to impress upon us the need which the theatre has of education, and the need which education has of the theatre. The beginnings of a general realization of this mutual need is one of the signs of our time. The fact that the L.C.C. recently decided that they could not afford Shakespeare performances for school-children is to be deplored; but the fact that they have recognized the possibility that Shakespeare performances might be good for school-children marks a big advance. It is not long since Mr. Charles T. Smith showed in *The School of Life* how successfully the drama could be made a part of elementary education, and that it is playing a very great and increasing part in higher education is plain to anybody who is in touch with the dramatic work now going on at the universities. Mr. Barker is very keen, and rightly so, that the students of his "theatre as school" should not specialize on their own subject to the detriment of their general education.

If, therefore, Mr. Barker had wished to "plan for the development of work already in being," instead of indulging his taste for castle-building, he would have found a good deal of material ready to his hand. It seems to me that the dramatic societies at Cambridge (to take the instance with which I happen to be most familiar) are actually doing work now which might serve as the firm terrestrial foundation of a real building very much like Mr. Granville-Barker's cloud-castle. The drama is gradually taking its proper place in the hierarchy of literature. In American universities courses of dramatic literature—that is, in playwriting—are already in being; and on what sound lines they are conducted the recently-published text-book on *Dramatic Technique*, by Professor G. P. Baker (of Harvard), will testify. We have not got as far as that yet in England, though progress in that direction is taking place. In the University of Liverpool there is a lectureship in Drama of which Mr. Granville-Barker himself was the first holder, and London University has followed suit (since the the publication of *The Exemplary Theatre*) by establishing a diploma to be awarded after a fairly comprehensive study, both theoretical and practical, of the theatre.

At the older Universities progress had been achieved by the efforts of individual enthusiasts rather than the powers that be. Sir Arthur Quiller-Couch, for instance, has succeeded in giving to English literature that honour in Cambridge which it should by rights have enjoyed long since. When he first occupied his chair in 1913, the study of English literature was confined to a miserable sub-section of the mediæval and modern languages Tripos; now it has a flourishing Tripos of its own. That represents so great a step forward that it seems quite reasonable to hope that students of English literature whose particular province is the drama will find themselves specially catered for within a measurable interval. On the acting and producing side the progress made in the same period has been extraordinary. The productions of the Marlowe Society and the A.D.C. have an importance and an "authority"—I am using the word in its French sense—that was quite lacking to their pre-war efforts. At Oxford exactly the same change is visible. The O.U.D.S. used to be a social club, with a slight bias towards acting. It is very different now.

At both Oxford and Cambridge real progress is hampered by the same trouble—lack of a theatre.

No big production can be staged at either place except by arrangement with the local playhouse. Such arrangements are difficult to make, and unsatisfactory when made. Rehearsals have to be carried on where and how they can. Experiment and study, of the kind which Mr. Granville-Barker wants to see, is barely possible. At Oxford the college halls have to serve for the less ambitious productions. Cambridge is slightly better off, since the A.D.C. has a theatre of its own, though it is far too small for the kind of work that is done in it.

And so, when I begin day-dreaming after Mr. Barker's fashion, I see every university in the country with its own theatre and its own school of drama—even, to some extent, of acting. But it seems to me much more important that would-be playwrights, critics, and producers should use a university school to get a knowledge of the practical side of the theatre than that the budding actors should crowd to it to be scientifically crammed with theory.

BACK TO METHUSELAH

WHEN I read *Back to Methuselah* in the light of the knowledge that I was about to see it produced in Birmingham I naturally made various conjectures as to how this or that part would "act." This is an impossible thing to do with certainty, even in the simple cases, and the case of what Mr. Bernard Shaw calls his "metabiological pentateuch" is far from simple. The work is written on two sharply contrasting themes. The first theme is one as great as can well be handled; the exposition of Mr. Shaw's passionate faith in the doctrine of creative evolution —that is, the belief that human life is at present too short for the needs of a complicated civilization, that man can only hope to save himself from the tragic mess that he has made of things by living longer and increasing his understanding, and, in fine, that he would be able, by an effort of what might be called his racial will, to extend the span of his life to Methuselah's and beyond, and so evolve a race of supermen. The second theme is trivial and personal, and consists of contemporary satire.

The ability of Mr. Shaw to get his laughs in the theatre by variations on the second theme I took for granted; but even allowing for the extraordinary theatrical virtuosity which has enabled him before now to make effective stage fabric out of raw materials which the ordinary playwright would never dream of handling at all, I arrived in Birmingham all prepared to be surprised if the fourth and fifth parts—and more particularly the latter—of *Back to Methuselah* did not prove better in the study than on the stage.

I was duly surprised. It is true that the caricatures of Mr. Lloyd George and Mr. Asquith in Part II and other little topical hits, for the purpose of making which Mr. Shaw allowed himself every now and then to step aside, got their laughs in due course. But it is also true that one felt it not so much a relief as a nuisance to be called upon to laugh at them. Compared now in retrospect with the engrossing interest of the last two parts, and with the magnificence of the close, the topical political satire has shrunk in my mind to the meanest proportions. In the second and third parts, it seems, Mr. Shaw is doing little more than working off his personal irritation against modern conditions, his personal contempt for the minds of the statesmen by whom we are ruled to-day and by whose counterparts—whatever may happen to be their political label or colour—we shall quite certainly be ruled to-morrow.

Dramatically, Mr. Shaw spends most of these two parts in "marking time." His main theme of creative evolution is starting, but has not yet got properly under way. He takes one whole play to relate the beginnings of the theory of longevity in A.D. 1920, and another to outline the beginnings of its practice in A.D. 2170. The material is rather thin to be spread out over so great a proportion of the whole work; he would have been better advised to make a single two-act play of it. His development of the idea that statesmen will never be really equal to the task of government till they live long enough to outgrow the game of party politics is, of course, germane to the chief theme; but the rest of these two parts is simply padding. Mr. Shaw turns aside deliberately to hold up his own particular virtues to us as forming an ideal state of grace towards which we must all strive, and to pour scorn upon Ministers so lost to a sense of their position as to occupy their spare time with non-Shavian pursuits such as golf,[1] bridge, love-making, and classical scholarship, or even to dare to have any spare time at all.

Part IV, *The Tragedy of an Elderly Gentleman*, brings us to something very different. Here the main theme moves ahead at full speed; Mr. Shaw is drawing a comparison between ourselves as we are and ourselves as creative evolution might make us in a thousand years. The serene contempt with which the long-livers regard the short-livers in this part makes dramatic fare immeasurably superior to the irritated contempt with which Mr. Shaw regarded the politicians in the former parts. The conversation between Zoo, the calm young woman of fifty-six, and Mr. Bluebin Barlow, O.M., the distracted elderly gentleman who visits the community of the long-livers, is magnificent comedy; in spite of the fact that

[1] For the benefit of his Cabinet Ministers two and a half centuries hence, Mr. Shaw has invented a game which he calls "marine golf." As an earnest and painstaking (though inefficient) golfer, I have tried without success to imagine what new horrors this grisly pastime may have in store for our descendants. What a pity that Mr. Shaw has not given us an account of a match.

this scene is one of the longest and longest-winded duologues ever written, it is so packed with ideas that it never flags for an instant.

I must say that I had little use after this for the second and third acts of this part—the Napoleon episode and the consultation of the Oracle. I wanted to know more about Zoo and Zozim and Fusima and the Oracle in their private lives and their relations with one another; all the time that we saw them they were too fully occupied in cheerfully despising Mr. Barlow and his friends to let us know much about themselves. Mr. Shaw might have given them a chance. In the last part he did elaborate his ideal community; but it was then too late for me—27,000 years too late. I should like to be one of the long-livers in A.D. 3000, but to be one of the oviparous humans of A.D. 30000, to have a mere four years of life in which to work off my appetite for love and beauty and art and games, before drying up into a sexless and solitary Ancient, whose sole and sufficient occupation for thousands of years is contemplation—that does not attract me at all. Still less does the further goal, as visualized by Mr. Shaw through the eyes of Lilith, attract me. I shrink from all these ultimate austerities like the short-liver I am.

Mr. Shaw knows just how I feel. He has put my instinctive revulsion from the whole state of ideal existence as he pictures it into the mouths of all his four-year-old oviparous artists and engineers and nymphs and swains, and he has no doubt put his reply to the criticism of me and such as me into the mouth of his He-Ancient—" Infant : One moment of the ecstasy of life as we live it would strike you dead." This answer does not move me; in my present unenlightened state I would rather be struck dead than be condemned to a perpetual old age which has outgrown the enjoyment of the senses but not their use. Perhaps I shall think differently in 27,000 years' time.

Meanwhile, the important point is this—that it is in this very part of his great drama, in which he denies what we know as beauty, that the beauty of Mr. Shaw's conception is most compelling. In the very act of stating that his work as a dramatic artist is nothing more than a child's amusement he has brought that work to a height that it has never before attained, by the sheer passion that is in him. That is, he has established his right to look behind and beyond our present ideas of beauty, by proving that he understands those ideas. Your pinchbeck reformer of the arts cannot work on this plane; he is driven to erect new qualities on the basis of his own defects—to pretend, for instance, that (because he himself cannot draw) every enlightened artist ought to despise drawing. Mr. Shaw has a wider vision than this; he knows that the only artist who may discard drawing is the man who has its technique at his fingers' ends.

There are in this immense, sprawling, and uneven work many blemishes that may be noted by the most casual eye. The influence of Mr. Shaw's own personal fads and aversions can be traced in it everywhere, but it is great drama all the same. That Mr. Shaw is a great man is an idea now pretty generally accepted among us, and we have had his own word on the point more than once. But if you want a proof of his stature you have it here in *Back to Methuselah*. It takes a great man to choose eternity as his theme and to handle it without making himself look small.

WAR PLAYS

THE fact that *Havoc* and *The Conquering Hero* were the first two serious plays about the war to be put before the London playgoing public had the natural effect of bracketing together these two pieces of work in our minds; but except for that single common factor in their composition they are as far asunder as the poles. There is no comparing them. *Havoc* is an excellent piece of dramatic writing, to which the close observation and faithful drawing of its war scenes have brought a great and well-deserved success with a public which had not hitherto been given the chance of seeing how the war looked on the stage. *The Conquering Hero* is a much bigger thing, both in design and in workmanship; in the issues with which it deals as well as the manner of its dealing with them.

Against Mr. Wall's now famous pictures of life as it was lived both behind and in the line by a a company of a battalion of infantry, Mr. Monkhouse has given us nothing but a single short act which is not realistic—by which I mean that it might just as easily have been written from hearsay or even from imagination as from first-hand knowledge; and yet *The Conquering Hero* is far more deeply concerned with the war than *Havoc.*

In the direct sense, Mr. Wall's characters are

not concerned with the war at all. Its war scenes are valuable, because they are closely observed and sincerely written; but take away the war setting, and the main story of the play remains—the story of the rivalry of two men for a worthless woman. It is a fact that the incidental war pictures quite outweigh the main story in importance and interest. It is true also that the war supplies a lurid background and a hectic atmosphere, and so gives credibility to a tale which in a more normal setting would have been mere melodrama. But for all that the war scenes *are* incidental, and supply nothing more than an atmosphere.

None of the men in Mr. Wall's play really thinks about the war at all; the attitude of each and every one of them, according to his temperament, is "Let us eat, drink, and be merry, for to-morrow we die." To each the war is simply a monstrous fact, to be accepted as a part of his ordinary routine, and to be made the best of as far as luck and a reasonably normal temperament will allow. Mr. Monkhouse deals with the outbreak of the war; his characters are caught at the moment when martial conditions are expected but not experienced, and the question of the war itself, its rights and its wrongs, occupies their minds to the exclusion of everything else. Most of them receive the news of Britain's entry into the struggle with enthusiasm; but to Chris Rokeby, the chief of them, war is not simply a fact to be accepted and made the best of. It is his attempt not to accept it at all that makes the play.

According to your understanding of the character of Chris you will like or dislike *The Conquering*

Hero, and in order to understand him you need to be able to look a little further beneath the surface than you are usually asked to do in the English theatre. On the surface Chris is, as his sister Margaret and Dakins the footman see him, a shirker and a coward; as Helen Thorburn sees him, a futile creature babbling of theories in a world suddenly grown practical; or as Iredale sees him, a well-meaning young man with an impossible point of view. Beneath that surface he is as Mr. Monkhouse sees him, a man cursed with a vision too clear for war-time, a man whose temperament is such that war leaves no place for him in the world.

Chris has the gift, fatal when a life and death struggle begins, of seeing both sides of a question; not one other character in the play labours under such a handicap. Consequently, in a group of ordinary honest human beings, each doing the right thing according to his lights, each showing courage in his own way, it is only Chris whose honesty is called in question, whose courage is taken for cowardice. He would give worlds to be like the rest, seeing his duty plain before him; but instead, his trouble of spirit drives him to cheap facetiousness and undignified brawling, and he loses even the appearance of sincerity.

Even when he has enlisted and been to the war, and won his sergeant's stripes, and been welcomed home by the village band (almost the only theatrical touch in the play) his uncompromising honesty, his too clear vision, must still defeat itself in the eyes of Chris's friends. He knows that he has done as well as the next man—which means that for a man of his temperament he has done supremely well; but he knows, also, that—as with the next man—his moments of heroism have been counterbalanced by moments of abject cowardice which—in common with the next man—he has managed to hide. His attempts to tell them honestly of this lead only to suspicions that he has done something disgraceful, to Helen's "Tell us what you've done—we can forgive," and Margaret's "I will be proud of you—if you'll let me."

But he does not let her. In his passion to put things before the others as he sees them he only succeeds in driving Margaret—the soldier's wife, the ardent militarist who is *plus royaliste que le roi*—to believe him guilty of "some horrible cowardice." There is more discernment in Helen's "We have done wrong. We should not have let you go"; but it is countered by Chris with "You mustn't judge things by their results. It was right to go. . . . The great man isn't crushed by war, not even by what I've gone through. If I'd been stronger—if I'd been better—it's very hard on men like me. This war is very hard on men like me." This play deserves to live, if only for the honesty and insight of its character-drawing; every person in it is a separate, living, human being—from the fine old Colonel, who never allows his passionate desire to see Chris a soldier to sway his son's decision, down through the main body of normal war-struck patriots to Dakins the footman.

All this is certainly hard going for the playgoer who likes to be allowed to stick to the surface of things—for people such as the lady who sat behind me on the first night, and proclaimed with a loud voice that it was all very well, but for her part she considered Chris a terrible rotter. This is the price Mr. Monkhouse pays for his admirable detachment.

Mr. Wall and Mr. Monkhouse have one quality in common—that they are both wise enough in their generation to concentrate the interest of their plays upon their characters. Mr. Hubert Griffith, in his *Tunnel Trench,* makes what I cannot but feel is an error in allowing the interest which he has aroused and sustained in his young Flying Corps officers to be dissipated and lost. Mr. Griffith has Mr. Monkhouse's intense seriousness about the war, and withal an acuteness of observation that has enabled him to do for the Flying Corps what Mr. Wall has done for the infantry.

Mr. Griffith's theme is a "successful" surprise attack along the British front, in which the advance is held up by obstinate fighting at a piece of line known as Tunnel Trench. We are shown the operations from various points of view—that of the Staff, of the infantry, of the Flying Corps—even from that of the Germans and the goddess Brynhilde. But the chief characters of the play are two young flying officers, Lieutenants Smith and St. Aubyn, respectively pilot and observer, between whom exists a friendship "passing the love of woman." The squadron to which they belong is engaged in contact patrol work over Tunnel Trench—that is, they are responsible for keeping Army Corps Headquarters informed of the progress made by the infantry. Smith and St. Aubyn are given the dangerous early morning job, when the barrage is at its most unpleasant, and come safely through. Later, however, the situation at Tunnel Trench being obscure, they are sent out again, and Smith is mortally wounded. St. Aubyn, half-crazed with grief, volunteers to go up once more as observer in the last patrol of the day with one Evelyn, a pilot whose intention is "to run my nose along that trench as low as ever I can go, barrage be damned." The machine is brought down just beside Tunnel Trench, and Evelyn is killed; but St. Aubyn, unhurt, crawls to a shell-hole, to find there his young brother, an infantry private, who dies in his arms.

This play has not shared the good fortune of the other two in being staged for a run in London; and as a fact, it seems to me to stand definitely below them in technical skill. The author has allowed his hatred of war to obsess him. Again and again he holds up the action of the play while he hammers home a nail that is already buried up to its head; and in consequence he has lost control of his theme. Indeed, he seems never to have made up his mind exactly what his theme is—whether the central figure of his play is St. Aubyn or Tunnel Trench. If the former, then much of the play is unnecessary, however great its intrinsic worth; if the latter, I feel that the author would have been better advised to follow more closely the method of Mr. Hardy in *The Dynasts* or of Mr. C. K. Munro in *The Rumour*—to include no characters so strongly drawn as to bulk larger in the eye of the spectator than the events in which they are taking part. In my view, however, Mr. Griffith would have done better to concentrate on his flying officers, for he has a real gift for the delineation of character, and he rises finely to his big moments.

The end of the play, as it stands in the printed text, illustrates very aptly the faults in its construction. Mr. Griffith has written, so to speak, two endings. The first is the scene where Brynhilde comes over the battlefield at night, seeking to carry to Valhalla those among the dead who have died in the old heroic belief in the glory of war, and finding, as she wanders over the plain, only one or two that are hers. The second is a short epilogue wherein the Army Corps Staff, with the weary lack of sentimentality born of custom, sum up the day's profit and loss. Either of these two widely different scenes might have brought the play effectively to a close, but superimposed upon the Brynhilde scene the epilogue appears to me sheer anti-climax. Something of the sort must have been discovered at rehearsal when the play was performed by one of the Sunday producing societies, for the Brynhilde scene was cut out—and cut out after the name of the actress who was to play the part had been publicly announced.

THE PLAY WITH A PURPOSE

EVERY good play has one main purpose, and only one—itself. That is a principle which should be clearly grasped and as clearly stated by every man who sets out to write about the theory of the theatre. There are not many points in the art of the playwright about which it is safe to dogmatize, not many rules which you can lay down without mental reservations; but here is one of the few. If a play is written not genuinely for the sake of the artist's joy in creation, but for some ulterior motive—which may in itself be praiseworthy or otherwise—its value as a play diminishes accordingly.

The play may be written because of the dramatist's desire to lay bare some social evil, or to set right some glaring injustice; or, quite simply, to make money; so long as the dramatist has greater interest in the characters he is creating and what happens to them, than in the abuses they are to symbolize or the money they are to make, all is yet well. The play will still be, according to the dramatist's ability, a good play. But as soon as it becomes manifest that an author has, consciously or unconsciously, subordinated his proper rôle of story-teller to that of preacher or advocate, his power has gone. The Play with a Purpose is branded the instant that its real nature shows itself.

Take, for example, Mr. Harold Owen's play,

Loyalty. This play, produced by the Vedrenne-Eadie management in 1917, was a very strong indictment of pacifist activities. It met—as was to be expected—with an enthusiastic reception in many quarters, but in spite of its patriotic purpose, it was severely handled by the dramatic critics, whose main objection was that the characters of the play were caricatures.

The author, in his preface to the published version of the play, speaks of this as "a criticism so demonstrably wide of the mark that—unable to compress the evidence against that view in this introduction—I have had to write a separate book altogether in order to show what pacifism really is and what sort of people pacifists really are." Whatever the rights of the case may have been the play ran for three weeks only, and since, at the time of its production, I was more closely concerned with the war itself than with plays about it, I did not myself know of the existence of *Loyalty* until I read it the other day.

Having done so, with the detachment that time has made possible, it seems to me that the play and the manner of its reception both bear out the theory stated above. I accept absolutely Mr. Owen's statement that he has drawn his group of pacifists straight from life; I believe without difficulty his further statement that he has given them queer clothes, squeaky voices, and narrow, fanatical minds because all the pacifists he has ever met were like that. After all, it is a very logical idea that cranks are likely to look, speak, and think like cranks, and that the people one meets who are cranky on one subject and normal on all others are exceptions to a rule. But all the same, I believe that by choosing these extreme types Mr. Owen threw away his best chance of making his play convincing. He drew from life his Stutchbury, his Ephraim Borer, his Stapleton Dunt, only to find the portraits derided as " incredible caricatures "— the reason being that every fanatic or extremist is an incredible creature to the normal man.

You know the tale of the old lady at the Zoo who regarded the giraffe for some moments and then remarked, " I simply don't believe it "? Well, that is your normal man's attitude when confronted with your crank. And so, when Mr. Owen opens his portrait gallery of pacifists and says to himself, " This will show up the cranks," the normal man says "Caricatures," and departs unimpressed.

The fact that Mr. Owen's is a tremendous and admirable purpose is not taken into consideration by the average playgoer, any more than the devotion of Dr. Marie Stopes to the doctrine of birth control saved her play *Our Ostriches* from being judged, and condemned, purely as drama. The fact is that by taking the extreme types of his opponents and heaping scorn upon them, the dramatist assures himself of preaching only to the converted. Those among his audience who possess the faculty of seeing both sides of a question at once suspect him of purposely laying on his colours too thick; and in consequence they either avoid his play, or else are influenced by it in exactly the wrong direction.

The only kind of Play with a Purpose that is convincing is the one which takes the best arguments of the opposite side, puts them into the mouths of partisans who are not extremists, and then proves them wrong. To me, the best anti-pacifist propaganda play is *The Conquering Hero.* This may surprise some worthy people, who think—if I understand them rightly—that Mr. Monkhouse's hero is a conscientious objector, whom it is the author's purpose to whitewash. I admit that I do not know what Mr. Monkhouse's opinions or his purposes are. It is his triumph in this play to have achieved so serene a detachment that you can say nothing for certain about him except that he has given you the facts and left you to draw from them what conclusions you will.

As I see it in this connection, *The Conquering Hero* is the story of a young man, gifted above his fellows with imagination, anxious only to do his duty, but lacking his fellows' simple certainty what that duty is. For a time he tries, and tries with real moral courage, to put into practice certain pacifist notions formed in a peaceful world; but he soons finds that in a world at war he is unable to make these notions work. He is not cut out for a soldier, but he joins up and does his best. (By the way, I wonder how many of the people who regard Chris Rokeby as a conscientous objector have noticed that he was in khaki by September, 1914, and in all probability—though the text does not settle this point—was in France in time to qualify for the 1914 medal?) He realizes, what the pacifist crank never will allow himself to realize, that when once a country has gone to war there is no longer any time or place for unpractical theories and ideals; the mere fact that the war has happened is a proof that those theories and ideals have failed. Even on his return, broken, Chris ratifies his new belief. "You mustn't judge things by their results," he says. "It was right to go. I have no regrets. How could I stay, while Frank and Stephen, and all the rest, were dying there? How could I see my father every day? And deep down in me—yes, deep—I'm an Englishman—all the old voices and the old tunes were calling." Mr. Monkhouse does not preach to the converted, because he is careful not to preach at all; but to my mind his analysis of the mind of Chris Rokeby contains far more damaging evidence against pacifism than Mr. Harold Owen's portrait gallery.

To a man with Mr. Owen's passionate sincerity and convictions, and his deep desire to show up and pillory these people whom he regards as traitors within the camp, I am afraid that this theory of mine with regard to propaganda plays must seem depressing in the extreme. The temptation to use the stage as a pulpit is tremendously strong, especially to a man who (like Mr. Owen) has a lesson he is burning to deliver, and the technical experience as a playwright to show him how to deliver it to the best effect. But theatre audiences dislike and resent above all things being preached at, even upon themes which touch their welfare most nearly; once let the theatre public have an inkling that it is being treated as a congregation by any dramatist, and it will show that dramatist very quickly what it thinks of sermons out of church.

This was very plainly brought home to me when I saw *So This is London*—a Play with a Purpose which demonstrated, in alternate slabs, how such a play should and should not be written. The purpose behind the play is the wholly excellent one of promoting a better mutual understanding between ourselves and America. The author's admirable idea was to take an average ignorant Englishman with an anti-American prejudice, and an average self-satisfied American with an anti-English bias, and to bring them together and show that they are brothers under their skins. He had a further brilliant inspiration—he staged two scenes showing the American's imaginary Englishman and the Englishman's imaginary American, and brought home to his audience the foolishness of these conceptions simply by throwing them into strong contrast with the real men about whom they had been formed.

All this the author did with an immense enjoyment of the dramatic qualities inherent in his story, an enjoyment which his audience found both delightful and infectious. If he had left it at that his auditors would have gone home chuckling over the play, and would have absorbed the underlying lesson unconsciously, probably announcing it to their home circles a day or two later as an original observation of their own.

Unfortunately, however, there were moments here and there when the sense of his message became too strong for the author. For this contingency he had in reserve one of his characters—an Anglo-American puppet; at such moments he would bring her forward and pull the string, and out would come propaganda. And the audience would sit, bored and resentful (I can answer for one unit of it, at least), but polite, until he should see fit to conclude his marionette interlude and get on with the play.

I remember similar attacks of resentment against

authors for the same reason. One lies in wait for me whenever I see Shaw's *The Dark Lady of the Sonnets.* In the very midst of my enjoyment of the dexterous dialogue between Shakespeare and Queen Elizabeth Mr. Shaw elbows the Virgin Queen on one side and treats me to an entirely irrelevant lecture on the national theatre question. His arguments are all very true, no doubt, and if I had gone to hear Mr. Shaw lecture on the subject I should in all probability agree with everything he said. But in the theatre I don't want it, and object to being forced to listen to it. The fact that the play was written for the express purpose of forcing me to listen to the lecture comforts me not at all. If that was all he was after, say I, he should not have written so well that he forced me to take an interest in the characters for their own sakes.

Of course, it takes a born dramatist to write well under such circumstances. The general characteristic of the authors of Plays with Purposes is that they write ecstatic rubbish. On one of my bookshelves I have a growing collection of astoundingly bad plays which have arrived for review in the ordinary course of events. It really is not possible to review these lucubrations—not, that is, at any greater length than half a dozen words, and reviews of that length (and of the necessary strength) would hardly escape editorial censure. I can only read, and marvel, and put them away on the shelf.

My collection is representative, I should say, of every possible kind and degree of badness. But the sheer heights of grotesque insanity are attainable only by writers of bad propaganda plays. When playwright turns propagandist the result, as I have said, is a play irritating to the audience and defective as a work of art; but when propagandist turns playwright the result must be seen to be believed. Your propagandist is by nature an enthusiast; and once it has occurred to him that the theatre is capable of being turned into a mighty engine for moulding public opinion he lets no petty questions of whether he can write a play disturb him. He sits down quickly and begins; and with a pen in his hand he runs presently mad.

I have specimens in this kind by people hardly literate; by people who, from their ideas of stage technique, do not seem to have been to a play since about 1870; by people who show no sign of ever having entered a theatre in their lives. All these people are blissfully unconscious that their performances fall in any way short of their intentions, as set forth in magniloquent and most impressive prefaces. Here is a typical example. One writer had conceived the idea—wholly creditable to himself, of course—of exposing the traffic in honours. He exposed it in a dull farce so cheap in texture, peopled by characters so drivelling, expressed in language so far removed from that of sane human beings, that the work was quite impossible to read to the end. And yet this author was able, in a readable and quite sensible preface, to make complacent reference to himself as "wielding this powerful weapon of ringing ridicule to slay a monster that has thrived so long and has very nearly demolished the fine fabric of public life in this country."

The fact is that no amount of fiery purpose will

make a playwright out of such an enthusiast. Unless a man can create living characters he cannot carry conviction on the stage. And the propagandist, as a rule, does not want his characters to have a separate life of their own, since it is his views, and his views only, that they exist to express. Of all the writers of Plays with a Purpose which have reached me in the past year or two, two only have realized the simple truth that if the play is to push home its message its characters must first be made to live. One is Miss Ruth Dodds, whose historical work, *The Pitman's Pay,* though written with an obvious propagandist purpose, and published by the Labour Publishing Company, is still worth its salt as drama; the other is Mr. Miles Malleson's *Conflict.*

TWO CRITICS

I CAN advance no really satisfactory reason for dealing in one article with *The Youngest Drama* by Mr. Ashley Dukes and *Drama and Mankind* by Mr. Halcott Glover. There are two likenesses between them, it is true; both books are published by Messrs. Ernest Benn, and each costs eight-and-sixpence. Otherwise, the only thing they have in common is their complete dissimilarity from one another.

Mr. Dukes's book has for sub-title *Studies of Fifty Dramatists;* but less than half of these can be called "youngest"—or even particularly young. Thirty are dealt with in one chapter under the general head of "Forerunners," and range from D'Annunzio to Zola. The order in which they are placed is alphabetical, but these two names serve well enough to fix the period covered by the whole chapter. After this come chapters on twenty-two modern writers (for Mr. Dukes has not allowed himself to be shackled by a mere title), subdivided as follows: Realists (St. John Ervine, C. K. Munro, Eugene O'Neill, Paul Richman, Charles Vildrac); Comedians (Fernand Crommelynk, Georges Duhamel, Sacha Guitry, A. A. Milne); Expressionists (Andreev, the Capeks, Georg Kaiser, Luigi Pirandello, Elmer Rice); Poets and Historians (Paul Claudel, John

Drinkwater, J. E. Flecker, Halcott Glover, Reinhard Sorge, Ernst Toller, Fritz von Unruh).

I give this list in full for two reasons. First, because it states in a straightforward way the scope and nature of Mr. Dukes's interests and knowledge; and secondly, because it illustrates clearly his method and design. To take these two aspects of his work separately, for the breadth of Mr. Dukes's interests and his knowledge I have nothing but admiration. Few critics, at all events few critics writing in English, could survey so wide a field with so nicely-balanced a judgment. He has brought to the reading and study—and, where possible, to the performance—of the plays with which he deals a mind singularly free from cant. He has no national axe to grind for use either for or against his own country's theatre. Because he admires modern German drama, that does not lead him to sneer at our own. Because he is writing of the newest drama, that does not lead him to conclude that the many of his "Forerunners" who are still writing no longer count. He is no apostle of a New Dawn; he is content to report certain signs he has discerned in the sky.

All this is very refreshing. Here for the first time you may see in their normal size and proportions figures which are usually presented to you through distorting mirrors. The Expressionists, for example. Generally these mysterious people are shown either (by their enemies) as lunatics or (by themselves) as supremely wise. Mr. Dukes presents them, on the same level and at the same distance as Messrs. St. John Ervine, A. A. Milne, and John Drinkwater, simply as dramatists; and he discusses their virtues and faults with the same detachment as he brings to the discussion of these other less disturbing writers.

And this brings me to my second point—Mr. Dukes's method and design. Against these I have a quarrel, which can be stated in one sentence. I feel that, given his interest in and knowledge of his subject, Mr. Dukes could, by adopting a different method, have written a very much more valuable book even than he has. He has dealt with each of his fifty-one dramatists (counting the Capeks as one) in a separate section to himself: each of these sections is witty, epigrammatic, discerning. Each of them hits off to a nicety Mr. Dukes's very carefully thought out and expressed opinion of its subject. But there is no connection between any one section and any other except the arbitrary one of grouping.

Nothing is so galling to an author as to be rapped over the knuckles for not writing a book which he never set out to write, but there it is. Mr. Dukes has all the materials here for a very fine piece of comparative analysis, instead of which he has compiled what somebody has described to me, not without justification, as a "Who's Who of Dramatists." When I first received this book and saw there was a chapter on the Expressionists, I said to myself, "At last! An article on Expressionism by somebody who isn't himself either an expressionist or a slayer of expressionists. I wonder what he makes of them!" Well, he doesn't attempt to make anything of them; he gives you little flashes of information about what an expressionist sets out to do—by the light of which we find that one man is an expressionist because he is not interested in drawing character, and another because he is interested in that to the exclusion of all else—but chiefly he occupies himself in setting before you little appreciations of the Capeks and others. And then I pick up an article by an expressionist author which denies with some heat that the Capeks can be called expressionists at all. It is most confusing.

Mr. Glover's book, so far from dealing in personalities, is so general in its nature that I cannot remember that anybody was mentioned by name in it at all—unless you count sundry characters from Dickens. (Having written this sentence, I open the volume at random at a place where Mr. Shaw's name occurs sixteen times in two pages. However, after a horror-stricken dash through the book I decide that this is an unlucky accident—that the original statement is near enough to the actual fact to be allowed to stand.)

Mr. Glover is, strictly speaking, a dramatist, not a critic, and since one of his beliefs is that the artist should not stray out of his own province into that of criticism, he makes it clear that he is writing neither as artist nor as critic, but simply as playgoer, His theme is a fine one; he is out to assert the paramount importance to the theatre of that much-abused entity, the public. He states firmly and dogmatically that theatrical art which does not appeal to the public is bad theatrical art, since "drama which does not appeal to a mass of men has failed as drama." His book is an immensely spirited outburst by a man who believes in drama, in humanity, and in life; who believes that modern drama does not deal directly enough with life; who believes, and is out to prove by logic, that "the poetic appeal is the only appeal that can reach masses of men"; that "there is nothing much wrong with the commercial manager, beyond his having been unduly impressed by the bore." Listen to this—which might be taken as a text for the whole:

> "You are horrified? You say I am making popularity a test of art? Well, I am—of the art of the theatre. It is the popular art par excellence. Who does not believe it does not believe in drama. But the matter is not as simple as it looks. Those qualities which ensure popularity must be present in every play. A good play does not stop at them. . . . A good dramatist is a host who sits with his guests, not a popular caterer who satisfies mere hunger at so much a head."

This is controversial stuff. Very many intellectual people will shy violently at the idea that those qualities that ensure popularity must be present in every play. What would the superior person do then, poor thing? But Mr. Glover has declared war on the superior person, and so far I believe he is right.

Naturally, a writer who describes his book as *A Vindication and a Challenge* is not going to carry any one man with him all the way. I find myself again and again agreeing with Mr. Glover on his main point, but dissenting from his corollaries. A single example may serve. Dealing with the function of criticism, Mr. Glover makes the exceedingly wise remark, "The test of a critic is what he likes, not what he condemns." Since nothing in this world is perfect, it is possible for any man possessed of a little smartness to pick holes in whatever good work you may place before him; indeed, many a small reputation for critical cleverness has been made on the strength of no other capacity than this. But then, having established his excellent point, Mr. Glover at once presses it too far:

> "Condemnation, however just by given standards, is invariably futile. It means simply that contact has not been effected. The square peg and the round hole. Anything that one man has been interested enough to say will be of interest to some man to hear, probably to many. Only the man who has been interested in that thing is competent to be its critic. If one is not that man, one had best be silent."

This, I think, is demonstrably wrong. It means, logically examined, that there is no such thing as bad art, or, if there is, that the man who likes bad art is the only man who should be allowed to judge it. I quite agree with Mr. Glover that if a man has a temperamental dislike for, say, farce, he would not in a perfect world be asked to criticize farces. But suppose a man, who has a liking for farces when they are good, goes to see a farce which plumbs the lowest depths of blithering imbecility to which writers in this kind are sometimes known to sink—what then? Is the critic to withhold his condemnation while he searches the lunatic asylums for somebody to praise the play?

THREE BARING PLAYS

It is long since there have been issued to the world under the same cover, and bearing the signature of the same author, three plays more dissimilar than those which make up the volume that lies before me.[1]

The plays have nothing whatever in common but the fact that they are all cast in dramatic form and divided up into acts and scenes. The first, *His Majesty's Embassy,* from which the book is christened, is a picture of life in the diplomatic service at any European capital. The second, *Manfroy, Duke of Athens,* is a romantic drama half in verse, half in prose, set in an unfamiliar mediæval Athens. The third, *June—And After*, is a modern light comedy beginning in Wimbledon and ending in Bryanston Square, which deals pleasantly enough with the matrimonial adventures and intrigues of a group of not very exciting people. About this last I do not propose to speak at any length. It is the kind of thing that a writer of Mr. Baring's distinction sometimes throws off because something about it happens to take his fancy; it is easily written and amusing, and may well be destined to find its way on to the stage of a London theatre. I should doubt if

[1] *His Majesty's Embassy,* by Maurice Baring (Heinemann).

either of the other plays in his book is likely to find a producer—unless, perhaps, one of them is put on by one of the producing societies for a special performance; but all the same, it is from these two plays that Mr. Baring's volume gets its importance.

His Majesty's Embassy abounds in admirable qualities. It is something very like a masterpiece in the art of capturing a special atmosphere; but it lacks one essential quality of the effective stage play—forward movement.

I remember when I was a small boy being taken to an exhibition at the Crystal Palace (I think) and shown an ant-hill, which was kept in some ingenious way under glass, so that you could look down and spy upon the private life of the ants. The insects continued about their business with no signs of embarrassment; but their business seldom kept them for any length of time on the surface. I found this very upsetting. Just as I got interested in any one particular ant and his doings he would dive down a subterranean passage and out of my life for ever; and I would have to find another object for my interest—who promptly behaved in the same way.

If only my selected insect had remained in that part of the ant-hill which was laid open to public inspection I should have been ready to stand and watch his goings-on all day, and be thrilled to the marrow. As it was I soon lost interest, and clamoured to be taken on to the next exhibit. I feel much the same now towards Mr. Baring's play. He takes the roof off his Embassy and shows us in detail exactly the kind of life its inmates lead—their different attitudes towards their diplomatic duties, their little social worries and strivings, their intrigues and philanderings. It is all amazingly cleverly done. But all the time I feel about Mr. Baring (as I did about my elders at that far-away exhibition) that he expects me to be interested chiefly in the ant-hill, while I want to follow the fortunes of individual ants; and once more I am troubled by their habit of disappearing from my ken just as my sympathies are aroused.

This does not disturb Mr. Baring in the least. "Look," he says, leaning over my shoulder and pointing. "That's the Ambassador, Sir Hedworth Lawless—that big one. He's very ill. That's his wife—the lady ant with him—but he doesn't love her a bit. He loves the other lady ant over there; Madame San Paolo her name is, the wife of the Italian First Secretary, who is beginning to be jealous. You can see him being jealous over there. Hallo, they've gone—I wonder what will become of them? . . . However, never mind. Come and look at this one. His name's Singleton. A bit of a bounder, between ourselves—trying to get on in his career by making love to useful women. There he goes—now look at this lot over here. . . ." And so on. After a little more of it I find my interest steadily slipping, especially as nothing very much does "become of them," even when they make their spasmodic reappearances. I am still full of admiration; but I go on with something like relief to the next exhibit.

Manfroy has just that quality of forward movement which *His Majesty's Embassy* lacks. Its hero, during its action, encounters every vicissitude of fortune from highest to lowest. At first he is the trusted favourite of the Duke of Athens; he is betrayed by false friends, and becomes a galley slave; he escapes and lives the life of an outlaw; then he is pardoned and becomes once more the Duke's favourite, and eventually his successor.

Throughout these trials and chances he keeps that quality which he most reveres in man—that quality which Macaulay found so admirable in Warren Hastings; a "noble equanimity, tried by both extremes of fortune, and never disturbed by either." But this quality in Manfroy is bound up with a self-sufficiency and a determination to fear not God nor regard man; and by reason of this evil streak in his character he yields to the temptation to dishonour the Princess Alathiel, whom chance has placed in his care; and it is by the consequences of this act that he is brought, twenty years later, to humble repentance and to death.

Here is a story told exactly after the manner of the Renaissance, and conforming closely to the Elizabethan dramatic traditions. If you were to compare it with the academic canons of Shakespearean tragedy as formulated by Professor Bradley, I believe you would find that it answers adequately enough to all the main requirements therein mentioned. It is, moreover, extremely well written (in spite of the carelessness which has omitted to correct such an astounding sentence as "It was another Alathiel; as beautiful as her ghost; and yet it was not her"). The verse has distinction, and rises in places to a high level of poetry. I must not therefore be understood to belittle its literary quality if I say that for stage purposes the play is no more than a sham antique.

It is not "sham" in the derogatory sense that it seeks merely to imitate an outworn mode; but in the more honourable sense that it attempts to make an old form fit a modern style. Elizabethan plays were written to fit the Elizabethan theatre and to appeal to the Elizabethan audience—a theatre and an audience vastly different from our own. There is a great deal of rather profitless worship of the Elizabethan stage and methods going on to-day, the outcome of which is more often valuable as a warning than as an example. Mr. William Archer devoted a great portion of his book, *The Old Drama and the New*, to what he called "The Elizabethan Legend," and made out a very complete case for his view that "the softness, the ductility, of the medium in which the Elizabethan dramatist worked, tended, not to the ennoblement, but to the cheapening of his product."

Mr. Archer had a good deal to say in his admirable book which no writer of the younger generation is likely to accept without argument; but the weight of evidence on this one point which he produced from the most praised works of the Elizabethans themselves was most impressive. If he had turned his microscope on to Mr. Baring's play he would, I think, have discovered additional evidence. He would have found, faithfully reproduced, most of those characteristics which he defined as faults inherent in the Elizabethan form; and I very much doubt if he would have found enough of the Elizabethan virtues to compensate him for the absence of the "more difficult and delicate art " which (he insists) the conditions of the modern theatre and the mentality of modern audiences have made of the drama. In other words, Mr. Baring has met the usual fate of those who seek to put new wine into old bottles.

THE "TRAGIC" COMEDIAN

IF the biography of William Schwenk Gilbert, by Mr. Sidney Dark and Miss Rowland Grey, had contained nothing else of note, our grateful thanks would still have been due to the authors for preserving to our enjoyment the beautiful example of local-paper criticism which dealt with an amateur performance of Gilbert's *Sweethearts*, arranged by the dramatist himself at Stanmore in 1904. "This comedy," said the writer, "which was first given in 1874, has lost nothing by keeping, and the little sketch was delightfully given. It is to be regretted that the comedies of Mr. Gilbert have undeservedly lost popularity in favour of the witty jingle wedded to the imperishable music of Sir Arthur Sullivan."

Heaven defend us! What a tale of cock and bull! It is, perhaps, only necessary to set side by side with this the remark of Mr. William Archer, who (in *The Old Drama and the New*), having allowed to Gilbert's earlier plays nothing more than "an unmistakable literary gift," marred by "a shallowness of thought, a hardness of style, and a cheapness of humour," goes on to say of the Gilbert and Sullivan operas that "in the history of the English theatre they will always hold an honoured place, for they helped, more than any other productions of their kind, to restore our national self-respect in matters of the theatre." When Mr. Maurice Baring, Mr. Walter Sichel, and Mr. Dark himself confidently bracket Gilbert's name with that of Aristophanes, it is not of his more serious work that they are thinking, any more than Professor Saintsbury, when he speaks of Gilbert's effect on the history of English prosody and his metrical kinship with the same Greek poet, is thinking of his blank verse.

In fact, there is only one distinguished man of letters to whom the unhappy chronicler of the Stanmore performance can look for approval, and that is Gilbert himself. "Gilbert," says Mr. Dark, "was frankly unable to understand the want of appreciation that his serious work received, at any rate after the eighties, and his lack of the power of self-criticism led him to suppose that critics were leagued against him, and that there was a conspiracy to prevent him from leaving the world which he had made all his own for a world which he would always have to share with others"; and, again: "The strangest and most ironic of Gilbertian paradoxes is that he never could realize that his serious plays were not equal to his magnificent excursions into the Land of Topsy-Turvydom." There is little room for doubt in Mr. Dark's other conclusion that Gilbert, as a rule, most detached and objective of writers, has given us one piece of autobiography—and autobiography with more than a touch of bitterness—in Jack Point.

"See," says Point, "I am a salaried wit; and is there aught in nature more ridiculous? A poor, dull, heart-broken man, who must needs be merry, or he will be whipped; who must rejoice, lest he starve; who must jest you, jibe you, quip you, crank you, wrack you, riddle you, from hour to hour, from day to day, from year to year, lest he dwindle, perish, starve, pine and die!"

Yes, there is bitterness here, and pathos; but the true pathos of the situation is not, surely, what Gilbert conceived it to be. The impulse that leads (or rather, drives) a man to express himself through the medium of humour, satire, or fantasy comes from the possession of a sense of proportion which is delicate above the ordinary; it is far more nearly allied to the critical than to the creative impulse. That is to say, the humorist is generally, like Jack Point, a man of serious and philosophic mind; and sooner or later his appreciation of what is deepest in literature breeds in him an aspiration to produce it for himself. But the two faculties are fundamentally different.

All art is the expression of emotion; but while the emotion expressed by the critic and the humorist is a sense of appreciation of life, the emotion expressed by the poet and the serious dramatist is a sense of life itself. The first has its roots in intellect, the second in passion. How far the two may be mutually destructive this is not the place to discuss; but an examination of Gilbert's work must surely lead to the conclusion that only at rare moments, if at all, had passionate emotion anything to do with its conception. In *Comedy and Tragedy,* for instance, he set out deliberately to express such an emotion, and achieved, by sheer technical skill, a theatrical tour de force—a vehicle for the passion of a fine tragic actress; to read *Comedy and Tragedy* thrills me not at all, but I am very ready to believe that to see it with Mary Anderson as Clarice was an unforgettable experience. Even in such moments of real pathos as Iolanthe's song,

> "He loves! If in the bygone years
> Thine eyes have ever shed
> Tears—bitter, unavailing tears
> For one untimely dead;
> If in the eventide of life
> Sad thoughts of her arise,
> Then let the memory of thy wife
> Plead for my boy—he dies!"

—even here the work is rather that of a clever technician who knows just how near he may go to sentimentality without slipping over the brink than of a poet. Only once is the detached and critical mind of the satirist carried away, and that is when, in drawing Jack Point, he draws a picture of himself yearning for the thing that is beyond his reach. The pathetic irony of the situation is not that he should have been compelled to jest when he wanted to preach, but that he should have failed to recognize that as a jester he actually stood higher than preaching could have carried him.

However, Mr. Dark overstates the case when he uses the word "tragedy" in this connection:

> "Gilbert was the most successful writer of comic opera libretti and of humorous verse that English literature has ever known. His work brought him wealth and immense popularity. He was quoted fifty times more frequently than half the poets dead and all the poets living. He found libretti vulgar doggerel, and left it a fine art, and it might

have been supposed that the consciousness of artistic achievement as well as material returns would have made him a happy man. But he was never quite happy, never really content."

It is not easy to feel that Gilbert suffered from anything more than that "divine discontent" which is the mark of the artist. There is a letter written by Gilbert to Sullivan, in which he discussses a suggestion that the two men should collaborate in a serious opera. Gilbert certainly refers his refusal to his belief that the public will take nothing from him but what is in essence humorous; but at the same time his first objection is put on a different basis: "To speak from my own selfish point of view, such an opera would afford me no chance of doing what I best do." He states his liking for a consistent story such as *The Yeomen* rather than the burlesquerie of more popular pieces such as *Iolanthe* or *The Mikado* (a preference which is shared by most good judges), but he shows no real desire to attempt anything more serious still, even apart from considerations of expediency. Nor is it the picture of a disappointed man that looks out at you from the various chapters of Mr. Dark's book. Neither in the man who for twenty years was the absolute autocrat of the Savoy stage, nor in the writer of the delightful letters (and, as his biographer says, "the real Gilbert is in his letters"); neither in the man whose pride in his professon is emphasized at every turn, nor in the owner of Grim's Dyke, the fine estate at Harrow Weald on which he loved to lavish his money, is there any real suggestion of the unfortunate who has tasted success only to find it turn to dust and ashes in his mouth. It is interesting to find him writing to Sullivan that " of the many substantial advantages that have resulted to me from our association " the most highly prized is to have written the libretto of the serious cantata, *The Martyr of Antioch;* it is interesting, moreover, to find him saying, " I fancy that posterity will know as little of me as I shall of posterity "; but no man can at any time be sure what posterity is going to think of him. And the last few years of his life must have given him some reason to change his mind. " It was not until Sullivan's death," says Mr. Dark, " that there was a general and conscious appreciation of the greatness of the gift that the two men had given to the English stage. Whole-hearted appreciation dates from 1906." Gilbert lived until 1911. If to have enjoyed such a life as his, to have died gallantly and instantaneously (he met his death by heart failure while trying to rescue a girl from drowning in his own lake) at the age of seventy-four, be tragedy, there are few of us who would not be glad to become tragic figures on the same terms.

THE SECRET LIFE

A NEW play from Mr. Harley Granville-Barker's pen is an event. When *The Secret Life* came into my hands I experienced a little thrill of anticipation, and sat down at once and read the play through—and made of it neither head nor tail. This, of course, is a manner of speaking; I understood it well enough to realize that I had been introduced to a group of brilliantly drawn characters—characters who were worth the careful craftsmanship and the depth of imagination that had gone to their fashioning; but I felt, as Mr. William Archer confessed that he always felt when reading *The Marrying of Ann Leete,* that the reasons for the sayings and doings of the characters were utterly enigmatic.

I was, however, not without hope that a second reading might shed light in the dark places; and when a fortnight later I sat down to the play again, I found to my joy and relief that this was so. In the light of my previous knowledge of the characters, the whole composition became—I will not say as clear as daylight, but clear enough to restore my confidence in my own ability to understand English. This second reading, with the wider comprehension it has brought me, confirms and deepens the impression made rather vaguely by the first—that here we have a piece of work right above and beyond the scope of most of our leading playwrights, but a piece of work so devoid of the fundamental stage virtue of clarity that I can hardly imagine that it could be successfully produced in the theatre except before an audience of people who, like me, had read the text through carefully twice before the curtain rose.

I write down clarity with confidence as a fundamental stage virtue; but since Mr Barker, who is one of the few really distinguished figures in the world of our theatre, has the habit of obscurity, I must show some cause for my confidence. It is obvious that if you talk to a man he will get little benefit from your conversation unless he understands what you are talking about. If he is (say) an intelligent farm-hand, and you happen to be talking about Greek roots, then you are simply a fool to have started a subject so far above his head; but even if your talk deals with roots of a more ordinary kind, of which you happen to have scientific and he only practical knowledge, you will still tell him nothing unless you tone down your scientific vocabulary to fit his practical comprehension. If you make your discourse clear to him, you send him back to cultivate his mangold-wurzels with a new fervour and a new knowledge; but if you make it clear only to yourself, you merely bemuse him and waste his time.

Mr. Granville-Barker in *The Secret Life* is not talking of anything so recondite as Greek roots, but of men and women very like ourselves. What he has to say is not beyond the comprehension of ordinary intelligent people, but his way of putting it is. It seems to me that the reason for his obscurity is due simply to the fact that he is concerned only to make his characters clear to himself, or, to put it another way, that he assumes in us the same inner knowledge of his characters that he himself possesses. He knows his characters too well, that is the truth of it. He has reached such a pitch of understanding with them that he can express them more fully to himself by what he implies than by what he actually says; and he expects us, who have only just met his people, to drop by instinct into the same happy intimacy with them. We cannot do it. Between Mr. Barker's attitude towards his characters and ours there is all the difference that distinguishes a pregnant silence between old friends from an uncomfortable silence between strangers. When we have read the play once or twice, our discomfort is dispelled. We are beginning to know these people, to appreciate their quality, to realize that they are worthy of Mr. Barker's intimacy. But isn't it then too late? Too late, I mean, for the playgoer who sees *The Secret Life* on the stage without having first read the text. He has to understand what Mr. Barker is getting at immediately or not at all; and it is to him, I take it, that every stage-play is addressed.

At this point, I expect, somebody will hurl a greater play than Mr. Barker's at my head. "What about *Hamlet?*" he will say. "There's obscurity for you, if you like. Why, people are arguing about it still. Am I to conclude that you think *Hamlet* a bad play?" Well, hardly. But there is a fundamental difference between the obscurity of Shakespeare and the obscurity of Mr. Barker. A playgoer unacquainted with the text of *Hamlet* would have no difficulty in understanding the main outlines of the tragedy, however puzzled he might be by its details; but I believe that he would be only too likely to come away from a performance of Mr. Barker's play puzzled not merely about details, but about the central theme. It would be no more to him than a disjointed tale of how Evan Strowde and Joan Westbury had loved one another in secret for eighteen years; how he had ruined his political career by brooding over the affair, while she did not allow it to interfere with the happiness of her married life; and how, when at last they were free to come together, they incomprehensibly decided to remain apart.

Not until he had got a thorough grasp of the characters of Evan and Joan could he begin to see the order behind this apparent chaos; till he had got that he would find his admiration for the quality of the writing tempered by a tantalizing realization that much fine detail was slipping past him unappreciated simply because he could not see how Mr. Barker's main structure hangs together. Coleridge once said that "poetry gives most pleasure when only generally and not perfectly understood." This remark gives, or at any rate implies, a reason why a man who would find pleasure again and again in the obscurities of *Hamlet* or of *The Cherry Orchard* might hesitate before tackling a second time the obscurities of *The Secret Life*.

I am not forgetting the very important possibility that these obscurities may tend to disappear when *The Secret Life* is produced. I am mindful of the words—already quoted in a previous essay—of the critic who confessed of *Hedda Gabler* that he could not make head or tail of it in the study, but found it as clear as crystal on the stage. Mr. Granville-Barker is as complete a man of the theatre as Ibsen; and one is tempted to assume that any play from his pen is bound to act more clearly than it reads. If I make no such assumption, it is because certain of the scenes in this play appear to have been specially designed to be difficult to grasp in the theatre.

The setting for Act II, for instance, is one end of a long gallery whose windows overlook a broad terrace. On this terrace, throughout the act, things happen. People play games on it, and argue on it, and hold lengthy conversations from it with other people in the gallery—being all the time, of course, quite invisible from the auditorium. There is one point at which Strowde and his sister Eleanor are carrying on a political conversation upstairs, while four other people are chattering below, discussing the origin and the rules of a local adaptation of the game of rounders, which they have just been playing on the terrace. Strowde has half an ear on the chatter, for he joins in it once, and refers to it later on; so we are manifestly intended to hear both conversations. All that the author says of this is that "the voices from below form a curious counterpoint" to the talk of Strowde and Eleanor; but I am quite convinced that no amount of care in production could make this scene intelligible to me. The remarks of unseen persons in the theatre are difficult enough to hear at the best of times; but when they form part of a contrapuntal scheme with the voices on the stage, I for one give the whole thing up as impossible. It would be foolish to make too much of this point, I admit; the scene is unimportant in itself, and, even if most of it goes by unheard, it will, no doubt, still have its value by giving the easy, friendly atmosphere of Braxted Abbey on a Sunday morning in summer. But, even so, it epitomizes the difficulty that I find with the whole play. Mr. Granville-Barker is himself so much at home in Braxted Abbey that he forgets that you and I are strangers to the house and don't know its ways.

THE OLD LADY

THE part of the *raisonneur*—the moralizing character who, without taking any very direct share in the action of a play, acted as a cross between showman and umpire to the chief characters—has ceased nowadays to be a regular item in the dramatist's stock-in-trade. But there seems to have been a tacit conspiracy between three of the best-known of our younger dramatists—to wit, Mr. John Drinkwater, Mr. St. John Ervine, and Mr. A. A. Milne—to restore this character to its former glory in the person of the Old Lady.

In Mr. Drinkwater's *Oliver Cromwell* quite the most attractive personage in the whole play is the Protector's mother, who is eighty when the play begins and ninety-five when it ends. In Mr. Ervine's *The Ship*, likewise, Old Mrs. Thurlow is the mother of the chief character; she is eighty-three, "but she has no intention of yielding to her years." In Mr. Milne's *The Lucky One*, Miss Farringdon is only a collateral relation, being great-aunt to the Farringdon brothers; here is her description: "She must be well over eighty. . . . She is very, very wise, and intensely interested in life."

There is something more than coincidence to account for this very marked resemblance between the three plays. Each of these three dramatists has had a theme to propound, and has needed a mouthpiece through which to propound his own comments on the actions of his characters; each has happened to see that an Old Lady suited his purpose better and more simply than any other character he could devise.

Mrs. Cromwell, Old Mrs. Thurlow, and Miss Farringdon are not so much three old ladies as three incarnations of the same Old Lady. She is a lady in the narrowest sense of the word—a gentlewoman; indeed, she has more than a touch of the *grande dame,* and her Shakespearean prototype is the Countess of Rousillon in *All's Well.* She is a clever woman, born in a generation in which women were given little encouragement to have brains, and none to use them for any purpose but the contemplation of life. That is why an Old Gentleman would not serve the same purpose at all; he would be far too eager to take part in whatever was going forward to achieve the Old Lady's Olympian detachment.

Her attitude towards the other characters of the play is exactly that of the author. Like him, she is concerned with, but not part of, the conflict which makes the drama; she does not take sides. Like him, she sits remote from and a little above the other people, regarding them with interest and love and deep understanding, but without passion. In the little world of his play the author is a god; and upon the Old Lady, sitting apart in her chair, descends the spirit of his godhead.

Mrs. Cromwell, set in the midst of civil turmoil, can see that her son is right to make war—and yet . . . " I sometimes think," she says, " the world isn't worth quarrelling about at all. And yet I'm a silly old woman to talk like that. But Oliver is a brave fellow—and John, all of them. I want them to be brave in peace—that's the way you think at eighty." And again, she asks her son what it will all come to. " There are times, mother, when we may not count the cost," he replies. Her answer is characteristic :

MRS. CROMWELL : You're very vexatious sometimes, Oliver.

CROMWELL : But you know I'm right in this, mother.

MRS. CROMWELL : Being right doesn't make you less vexatious.

But perhaps no single sentence she speaks is so illuminating as her epitaph on Charles I, spoken when she hears the news that the execution is over : " Poor, silly king."

Old Mrs. Thurlow is a more conscious philosopher. Her mission in life is to hold the balance true between her son, the shipbuilder, and his son, who hates machinery and wants to go back to the land. First, you find her defending the father to the son :

People like your father haven't finished their work, they're only midway through it. But you think, because you see the confusion of a half-completed job, that it's a bungled job. You said something just now about the bitterness which fills the young men who come back from the war, but you don't seem to realize that an ideal which cannot survive a blow——

JACK : A terrible blow, granny.

OLD MRS. THURLOW : Yes, dear, a very terrible blow, but surely the only ideal worth having is one which survives all blows? To me, the most wonderful thing in the world is not the young man beginning life with ideals—we all do that—but the old man dying with them undiminished.

But soon after you find her defending the son to the father:

It's foolish, my dear, to force the wrong views on the right people.

She is not afraid, either, to act according to her philosophy:

It's very wrong to make people do things they don't want to do, even when those things are right. . . . Your views, Jack, are rather silly, but no one can make you realize how silly they are so well as you can. It is a pity you don't like ships . . . but since you don't, and your father won't give you the money to buy your farm, I'm afraid I shall have to give it you.

And in another passage she actually states the author's point of view in so many words.

A granny has all the pleasures of motherhood without any of the pains. . . . You are my ships, all of you, going out on long, difficult journeys to strange places, little ships and big ships that I made, that I love.

Miss Farringdon is a little different from the other two. You feel about Mrs. Cromwell and Mrs. Thurlow that any mistakes they might make would be the mistakes of Mr. Drinkwater or Mr. Ervine. Mr. Milne, on the other hand, allows Miss Farringdon to make one bad mistake on her own account; for two acts out of three she misjudges the character of her nephew Gerald. But she is none the less the author's mouthpiece; the whole point of this play, *The Lucky One*, lies in the revelation that Gerald, the brilliant and charming and superficial younger brother, is not really superficial at all; and that when he loses Pamela to Bob (the less attractive elder brother) he loses something for which no other success can make up to him. And so for two acts Mr. Milne deliberately deceives his audience. The reader instinctively assumes that Miss Farringdon's view is the correct one; and there is hardly a scrap of evidence to prepare us for Gerald's emergence in his true colours. It is true that Gerald himself lets fall an occasional hint that he is not as superficial as he seems—that there are hidden depths beneath. But then, you can hardly expect a clever, superficial man to admit (or even realize) his superficiality. I believe that this unexpected change of attitude on the part of Mr. Milne is responsible for the fact that *The Lucky One*, alone of Mr. Milne's first plays, has not been seen on the regular stage. The author confesses that he thinks it the best play in his first volume, but doomed from the beginning because "the girl marries the wrong man." But I believe that if he had made it clear to the audience (through Miss Farringdon) which the right man really was, the lack of a conventional happy ending wouldn't have mattered. And the part of Gerald would have suited Mr. Owen Nares better than anything he has done.

STUDIO PLAYS

Mr. Clifford Bax has a hankering after minuteness of workmanship. If his talents had happened to lie in some other direction than literary composition, he would probably have become known to fame for engraving the alphabet on the head of a pin, or something like that. As it is, he delights in turning out plays of incredible conciseness. His *Midsummer Madness,* produced by Mr. Playfair, was chiefly remarkable for the manner in which the author, with only four characters, and disdaining the aid of anything so robust as a plot, managed to produce a three-act play which actually scored a success. Personally, I prefer the miniature version of this play which he has since published under the title of *Nocturne in Palermo.* This has five characters, but only one act; and the length seems to me to suit Mr. Bax's gentle irony and eye for the picturesque, while not tempting him to stretch a tenuous thread of story beyond its strength.

Mr. Bax has many stage miniatures to his credit, best of which, I think, is *Prelude and Fugue.* This was published as one of a series of three Studio Plays; but some considerable time before it appeared in print I was one of a small audience which assembled in a studio to see this play performed, and it impressed me strongly as a most interesting experiment in dramatic technique.

It is written in blank verse, and its only characters are two girls, Joan and Rosemary, respectively artist and sitter. It begins with desultory conversation, while Joan works on her picture. It appears that Rosemary is very soon to be married, while Joan is only waiting till the picture is finished to start for Spain. The name of one Philip Hardy crops up, and the talk at once ceases to be desultory, though it is more spasmodic than ever. But you may judge for yourselves—here is the passage:

ROSEMARY: Yes—but who told you?
JOAN: Someone . . . a friend of yours . . .
(Bother these chalks).
[*She breaks a pastel and stoops to pick it up.*]
A man named Philip Hardy.
ROSEMARY: A "friend" of mine!
JOAN: Or so I understood. Isn't he?
ROSEMARY (*quietly*): No.
[*A pause.*]
Do you know Philip Hardy—well, I mean?
JOAN: Fairly.
ROSEMARY: You like him?
JOAN: Oh, I like him—yes.
[*A pause. Joan smiles at her thoughts.*]
ROSEMARY: Why are you smiling? A penny for your thoughts!
JOAN: Was I? How funny . . . I really don't know why.
[*A pause.*]
ROSEMARY: Did he say much about me?
JOAN: Who? You mean
Philip? Not much; but somehow, all the same,
I had the impression that he knows you well.
[*A longer pause.*]
So that's that! Now you're free.

The significance of this, you see, is all in the pauses. It is clear enough that Rosemary knows something about Philip Hardy, and that she does not like him. Joan's feelings are less easy to fathom; but she is obviously following out some train of thought which Rosemary's words have set going in her mind. Meanwhile, the picture is finished. The two girls examine and discuss it; Rosemary declines an invitation to tea, puts on her cloak, says good-bye; but on her way to the door she stops to examine a little Roman lamp on a table. Joan is tidying away her chalks, but suddenly she turns round and flings out the blunt question: "What did you mean?" And the little scene works to its conclusion thus:

ROSEMARY (*looking her in the eyes*):
I'm sorry for any girl
Who finds out that she's loved a drunken beast.
[*Joan half turns away.*]
JOAN (*facing Rosemary again*):
You can't know Philip Hardy very well,
Talking such nonsense. I don't mind, not a bit.
ROSEMARY: I spoke the truth about him. And I know.
[*Joan takes off her overall.*]
JOAN: And what's more, I'm astonished that anyone
Like you, should credit a silly tale like that.
ROSEMARY: Can't you guess how I know? It's not a tale.
[*A pause. Joan lays the overall on Rosemary's chair.*]
ROSEMARY (*holding out her hand*):
Good-bye. You sail—to-morrow?
JOAN: Did you say
Your wedding falls on Tuesday of next week?
ROSEMARY: Yes.
JOAN (*taking her hand*): May I come?
ROSEMARY: No need to answer that.

At this point out go the lights, and you are left (or perhaps I had better say I was left) literally as well as figuratively very much in the dark. You have been shown a moment of importance in the lives of two people, arising suddenly out of nothing, as such moments will. It is a moment full of significance to the two people who are living it; but for you, the outsider, the eavesdropper, it has gone by before you have had time to grasp more than a fraction of that significance. You sit there in the darkness, and the germ of an indignation against Mr. Clifford Bax stirs within you.

But here the lights go up again, and in another minute or two you realize that the man knows what he is doing after all. Joan is back at her easel, Rosemary in her chair; and they are beginning once again their desultory conversation concerning an imminent wedding and a journey to Spain. But there is a difference, for now, instead of the pauses, we have soliloquies in which each girl speaks her thoughts. At once the disjointed scraps of dialogue begin to fit themselves into place. For instance, the passage first quoted above now runs thus:

JOAN: A man named Philip Hardy.
ROSEMARY: A " friend " of mine!
JOAN: Or so I understood. Isn't he?
ROSEMARY (*quietly*): No.

. . . .

JOAN: How queer—she doesn't like him! What can it mean?
Phil certainly talked as though they were good friends.
What can she have against him? If I ask
She'll guess how much I care.

ROSEMARY: Philip and she
Acquainted! What on earth should I have done
If we had met here? Goodness only knows. . . .
But, anyway, he was gentleman enough
Not to say much, not to have thrown out hints,
Even, that he once had me nearly crazed.
I know why, too—that would have queered his pitch.
He wants to fool her as he once fooled me.

. . . . . .

Do you know Philip Hardy—well, I mean?
JOAN: Fairly.
ROSEMARY: You like him!
JOAN: Oh, I like him—yes.

. . . .

ROSEMARY: She can't know much about him: but then, of course
No satyr ever parades the cloven hoof,
And Philip's a well-dressed devil and debonair,
And nobody could resist him at the start.
JOAN: What can have made her deny him as a friend?
Nothing . . . some dreary scandal about his past,
About some woman. She'd probably be shocked
By what amuses *me*. I'd not give much
For any man of forty who had no past!
[*She smiles at her thoughts.*]

And so the scene goes on—clear as daylight now. From Joan we learn that it is with Philip Hardy that she is going to Spain for "a month's romance, an unblessed love affair, a madcap jaunt with someone whom I have known for nineteen days"; from Rosemary, that she is debating within herself whether to utter a warning and the confession which is implied therein. As the scene develops, you find Joan's abrupt question, "What did you mean," and Rosemary's uncompromising answer, satisfying instead of disturbing to your mind; and Joan's quick denial and subsequent acceptance of the statement that Philip is "a drunken beast" follow as naturally as her final tacit decision to go to Rosemary's wedding instead of to Spain.

I am not going to pretend that I think this play will appeal to everybody as it did to me. In *Prelude and Fugue* Mr. Bax is talking only to that comparatively small section of the public which finds the method of a story-teller even more engrossing than his matter. The average playgoer is not interested in dramatic technique. He finds it trying enough to be told a muddled story the first time, and is certainly not likely to sit quiet while Mr. Bax goes over it again with annotations.

The lights go out after the first scene. "Ah!" says Mr. Bax, like some professor of literary legerdemain, "you didn't see how that happened, did you? Now, watch me carefully. . . ." The incident happens again in slow time, and the average playgoer, rising indignantly from his seat (or, more probably, since we are in a studio, from the floor), departs in disgust, saying that if he wants that kind of thing he can go to Maskelyne's for it. But Mr. Bax's select audience of people who like to see "how it's done," and who consider that original experimental work of this and every other kind is what our theatre most needs, remains to applaud and ask him eagerly for more.